# THE
# MESSIANIC
# ANSWER
# BOOK

Jewish ANSWERS
To Jewish QUESTIONS
About THE Jewish Messiah

## SAM NADLER

REVISED AND EXPANDED EDITION

Note to the Reader:

Throughout the text, the name "Yeshua" is used to refer to Jesus. It is His Hebrew name.

Where a second verse is given in brackets (for example, Isaiah 9:6[5]), the first verse refers to the English numbering, and the second to the Hebrew.

Shalom Fellow Seekers,

I hope that as you find answers to your questions, you will come to know Messiah, who is the very Truth of God. May many more come to know joy and forgiveness because of what you read.

Sam Nadler

# TABLE OF CONTENTS

# AN INTRODUCTION of SORTS:
## A STORY of QUESTIONS and FAITH

Though I grew up in a loving Orthodox Jewish home, religion was always a mystery to me. "Jewish" was who we were, not merely what we practiced or believed. Still, I couldn't quite understand God. I had many questions about the Holocaust, birth defects, unsolved crimes and other seeming contradictions to the idea of a God-ordered universe. There didn't seem to be any objective information for me to consider. So after my bar mitzvah (like a confirmation ceremony, but with chopped liver) I felt disinclined toward further religious involvement.

Following my stint in Vietnam, I lived in various scenic locales of California, the "promised land" of broken promises for my generation. It was there that I ran into Jewish believers in Jesus, and felt sorry for them. One thing any Jew should know is that Jews do not believe in Jesus.

However, after looking into it for myself, I got the uncomfortable feeling that there was more objective information on the matter than I previously thought. In fact, when I first read Isaiah 53 (see pages 124-127) I was shocked. I figured that those sneaky Christians had stuck a portion of their New Testament into my side of the Bible! Nothing was supposed to be that clear.

After several months of further investigation I became convinced of two things. First, there is such a thing as spiritual evil—until that time I had figured there was no objective right and wrong. Eastern religion, meditation, and drugs were opening me up spiritually—but to the wrong spirit. If there was a spiritual battle for my soul, I was losing was on the losing side. Second, the Scriptures convinced me that Yeshua is the Messiah of Israel, the Savior I desperately needed. Though I didn't know all the right words to say, I asked Yeshua to save me. And He did. When I prayed to Him, I was cleansed from my sins, forgiven, and I experienced a peace that I had never known before—a peace that passes all understanding.

The Lord was gracious to me, an ordinary sinner, and I was assured that He Himself is the answer for my life, and the lives of all my people. To this day I still have questions, but many of my initial objections were answered by the facts of who Yeshua is according to the Scriptures. Throughout this book we will refer both to the Hebrew Scriptures and the New Testament (or New Covenant, from Jeremiah 31:31).

In the back of this book are additional stories of faith written by Jewish people—a Holocaust survivor, a professional musician, a housewife and mother, a businessman, and others—who have found the answer in Messiah Yeshua.

Some of the questions included in this book may be your questions as well. In which case, enjoy yourself, and perhaps you can come up with a few more for me to work through with you. In any case, here are some of the most often asked questions from our people regarding faith in Yeshua as the Messiah.

Sam Nadler

# ONE

# HOW CAN A JEW BELIEVE IN JESUS AND STILL BE JEWISH?

It all depends on who Yeshua is! The New Covenant presents Yeshua as the Jewish Messiah (John 1:41, 45, 49, etc.). If He's not the Jewish Messiah then no one should believe in Him, because His credentials as Savior of the World are based on His credentials as the Messiah of Israel. If He is the true Messiah, then it is kosher that I as a Jewish person believe in Him. And I would be a Jew in good standing with God, even if no one else agreed.

For argument's sake, suppose that Yeshua is a false Messiah. In the eyes of rabbinical authority I must still be seen as a Jew. Why? Because believing in a false messiah does not make any Jew a non-Jew.

For example, in 132 CE, the rebel leader Simon bar Kochba arose during the Jewish revolt against Rome. Rabbi Akiva (a very famous rabbi) declared Bar Kochba to be the

Messiah, although at the time Bar Kochba had none of the accepted credentials. The declaration appears to have been a pragmatic attempt on Rabbi Akiva's part to unite the Jews against Rome. However, no Jewish authority has ever said, "Akiva is no longer Jewish for believing in a false messiah."

If, after endorsing a false messiah, Rabbi Akiva is still considered to be a Jew in good standing, then one who believes Yeshua is Messiah cannot be considered otherwise.

In a synagogue on Long Island, New York, I once had the opportunity to give a presentation on why I believed Yeshua is the Messiah. Afterward, the senior rabbi stood up and declared, "Nadler, you're no longer a Jew because of your belief in Jesus!"

"Rabbi," I responded, "If the Bostoner Rebbe says I'm still a Jew, though a wayward one, and if the Encyclopedia Judaica declares I'm still a Jew, though a wayward one, then on what basis can you say I'm no longer a Jew?" "Well," the rabbi said, "perhaps I'm wrong." "Rabbi," I quietly responded, "maybe you're wrong about more than just that?" To my astonishment, the synagogue audience of over a hundred Jewish people erupted into applause. It was apparent to all who would consider the issues objectively that a Jew who believes in Yeshua is still a Jew, whether the rabbi approves or not.

## JEWISH IDENTITY REMAINS

In the New Covenant book of John the early believers in Yeshua described him as: "the Messiah"; "the One spoken of in Moses and the Prophets"; "the King of Israel"; and so on. They consistently saw Yeshua in a Jewish frame of reference, as the centerpiece of Jewish history.

Please notice also how these believers understood themselves. In both Acts 21:39 and 22:3 in the New Covenant, Paul declares first to the Romans, then again to his own Jewish people, "I am a Jew from Tarsus." Now at this time, Paul had been a believer in Yeshua for well over twenty years. So it isn't that he's confused or that he's trying to say one thing to the Romans, and something else to the Jews. Paul doesn't say that he "was a Jew," "an ex-Jew from Tarsus," or a "former Jew," etc.—Paul considered himself a present-tense Jew.

## Why "Still Being Jewish" Matters

In Romans 11:1, Paul reiterates his Jewish identity when he raises the rhetorical question, "Has God forsaken His people (Israel)?" He then answers, "Not at all! For I am an Israelite, of the seed of Abraham, of the tribe of Benjamin." His first "proof" that God has not forsaken Israel is himself. God chose a "Hebrew of Hebrews" (Phil. 3:5) so that the Gentile world would never think that God would forsake "a people whom He foreknew."

Today it's the same story. Every Jewish believer living his or her present-tense Jewish identity testifies, "*Am Yisrael Chai b'Yeshua HaMashiach!*" - The people of Israel live in Yeshua the Messiah! For if the Lord would break His promises to Israel, why should anyone else think Him trustworthy regarding the Good News of Yeshua?

Many people, both Jewish and Gentile, are unaware that the New Covenant does not restrict in any fashion Jewish believers from identifying and living as Jews. Yes, coming to faith in Messiah Yeshua is a radical change, a heart transformation of turning from sin and to God. That said, the New Covenant only builds upon and fulfills the ethical, moral and spiritual teaching and revelation of

God in the Hebrew Scriptures. So, in the New Covenant we read that the early believers continued attending the Temple and synagogue, kept the feasts, circumcised their Jewish children, and kept other aspects of the Law. This was not to deny Messiah's authority or to show they merited righteousness, but for the sake of identifying with their own people and honoring the Lord. In short, they remained Jewish (Acts 3; 20:6, 16; 1 Cor. 16:8; Acts 16:1-3; Matt. 11:29; Acts 15:10).

## UNITY, NOT UNIFORMITY

Unfortunately, because of church history, there's a lot of "stinking thinking" on this subject, even among Christians. A few years back, I was invited to speak on a secular radio call-in show in Miami, Florida. I received a number of "you're-no-longer-a-Jew" calls from Jewish listeners. Then a call came in from a more polite gentleman: "Mr. Nadler, now that you're a believer in Jesus you're no longer a Jew, for the Bible says that 'in Messiah there's neither Jew nor Greek.'"

I recognized the Scripture portion and responded over the air, "Oh, you mean Galatians 3:28, 'there's neither Jew nor Greek, bond nor free, male nor female; for we are all one in Messiah Jesus'."

"Exactly," the caller replied.

"Then let me ask you a question. Are you a believer?"

"Yes, I am," he answered.

"Great. Are you married?" I asked.

"Well, yes, I'm married," he slowly answered.

"Is your wife a believer?"

"Yes, she's a believer," he responded after a longer pause.

"Well," I said, pausing to catch my breath. "If you're a believer and still a male, and your wife is a believer and still a female, then I'm a believer and still a Jew. The verse in Galatians is not teaching that we lose our identities in Messiah, but that there's only one way to God for all people."

An extremely long pause, then "You mean... I'm still Jewish?"

"If you were born a Jew," I responded, "then you're still a Jew."

"Hallelujah!" he shouted over the airwaves, "They told me I was no longer Jewish."

Yes, it has been said that one cannot believe in Jesus and still be Jewish. If however, Yeshua is our Messiah as the Bible teaches, then trusting in Him is the most Jewish decision one can ever make!

# TWO

# IF I CAN GO DIRECTLY TO GOD, WHY DO I NEED A MEDIATOR?

The apocryphal story is told of US President Ronald Reagan showing Israeli Prime Minister Menachem Begin his phone service in Washington.

"This red one is the hotline to Moscow, this 'blackbox' is for nuclear war;" then with a flourish Reagan said, "but this gold phone is a direct line right to the Pope himself!"

Later in Jerusalem, Begin showed Reagan his communication devices.

"This red phone is a hotline to Egypt, this blue phone is to call out the troops." Begin paused, and then pointing to an ordinary looking black phone he said, "that one's for spiritual matters."

"Oh, really," Reagan said, "and who does that phone reach?"

## CHAPTER TWO

## PROMISED MEDIATION FOR ISRAEL

In fact, both the priesthood and prophetic intercession pointed in three ways to a future mediator for Israel. First, God would not provide revelation directly to each Israelite, but rather through a prophet like Moses:

> "The LORD your God will raise up for you a prophet like me from among your countrymen. You shall listen to him." (Deuteronomy 18:15, ca.1400 BCE)

> נָבִיא מִקִּרְבְּךָ מֵאַחֶיךָ כָּמֹנִי
> יָקִים לְךָ יְיָ אֱלֹהֶיךָ
> אֵלָיו תִּשְׁמָעוּן:

This way each would not "hear the voice of the LORD" and surely die (Deut. 18:16). This text was seen to point to Messiah. He would be "a light for the Gentiles" and "a covenant for the people" (Isaiah 49:5-8).

Second, God had promised an eternal priesthood, which originates with Messiah, and which is foreshadowed by the Levitical priesthood:

> The LORD has sworn and will not change His mind: "You [Messiah] are a priest forever, in the order of Melchizedek" (Psalm 110:4, ca. 1000 BCE)

> נִשְׁבַּע יְהוָה וְלֹא יִנָּחֵם
> אַתָּה־כֹהֵן לְעוֹלָם
> עַל־דִּבְרָתִי מַלְכִּי־צֶדֶק:

The people would never be left without priestly mediation, as His will is that we would have a proper way to draw near to Him.

Third, God promised to provide a perfect intercession for transgressors in the Messiah:

> He will divide the spoils with the strong, because He [Messiah] poured Himself out unto death, and was numbered with the transgressors; for He bore the sin of many, and made intercession for the transgressors. (Isaiah 53:12, ca. 700 BCE)

Messiah would be the perfect sacrifice for sins, as "He bore the sin of many." Therefore as our mediator He would be able to provide perfect intercession for all who trust in God through Him.

## Provided Mediation For Israel

With both the past and predicted mediation taught in the Jewish Scriptures, God has fulfilled His Word and Messiah has come! When Yeshua taught His followers, "I am the way and the truth and the life; no one comes to the Father but by Me," He was declaring what was to be expected from the true Messiah, our Mediator (John 14:6). In accordance with the principles of the rest of the Jewish Scriptures, the writer of Hebrews states:

> ...it is declared: "You are a priest forever, in the order of Melchizedek." Because Yeshua lives forever, He has a permanent priesthood. Therefore He is able to save completely those who draw near to God through Him, because He always lives to make intercession for them (Hebrews 7:17, 24, 25).

The fulfillment of this need for mediation, promised by the God of Israel, and foreshadowed by Moses, David and Isaiah, has come. The Messiah of Israel is ready to intercede for those who will turn to Him, allowing them to "draw near to God through Him."

# THREE

# DOESN'T KEEPING THE LAW KEEP ME RIGHT WITH GOD?

W e have considered how Jewish believers in Messiah, as recorded in the New Covenant Scriptures, were faithful to God in how they lived, and that they did nothing to contradict the Law of Moses. However, there is a common misconception about why the Law was given, namely, that Jewish people merit righteousness before God by keeping it. In other words, some believe that salvation through Messiah is unnecessary because we are made righteous by keeping the Law. This is close, as the saying goes, but no cigar.

## THE PREMISE OF THE LAW

Yes, the Jewish people have been chosen for a divine purpose. However, the Law was given to reveal God's holiness, not ours. It was given to demonstrate His love, not our worthiness to receive love. In fact, the Law of Moses found in the Torah is actually a conditional covenant, or agreement. Notice what God stated when the Law was given:

> "Now therefore if you will obey my voice indeed, and keep my covenant, then you will be a special treasure to Me above all the people; for all the earth is mine." (Exodus 19:5)

וְעַתָּה אִם־שָׁמוֹעַ תִּשְׁמְעוּ בְּקֹלִי
וּשְׁמַרְתֶּם אֶת־בְּרִיתִי וִהְיִיתֶם לִי
סְגֻלָּה מִכָּל־הָעַמִּים כִּי־לִי כָּל־הָאָרֶץ:

Notice the underlined words in the passage below, which reiterates the same idea.

> "And it shall come to pass, if you will listen diligently to the voice of the LORD your God, to observe and do all His commandments which I command you this day, then the LORD your God will set you high above all the nations of the earth. And all these blessings shall come on you, and overtake you, if you shall heed the voice of the LORD your God." (Deuteronomy 28:1-2)

וְהָיָה אִם־שָׁמוֹעַ תִּשְׁמַע
בְּקוֹל יְיָ אֱלֹהֶיךָ לִשְׁמֹר לַעֲשׂוֹת
אֶת־כָּל־מִצְוֹתָיו אֲשֶׁר אָנֹכִי מְצַוְּךָ הַיּוֹם
וּנְתָנְךָ יְיָ אֱלֹהֶיךָ עֶלְיוֹן עַל כָּל־גּוֹיֵי הָאָרֶץ:
וּבָאוּ עָלֶיךָ כָּל־הַבְּרָכוֹת הָאֵלֶּה וְהִשִּׂיגֻךָ
כִּי תִשְׁמַע בְּקוֹל יְיָ אֱלֹהֶיךָ:

These statements are followed by twelve verses of blessings. Once more the words "if" and "then" are underlined. These words describe a conditional covenant or agreement. The phrase "conditional covenant" means that the benefits are received if the conditions are met.

The condition is not piecemeal observance, but following the whole thing. Suppose I said to my son, "*if* you clean your room, *then* I will give you a dollar." If he didn't clean his room, he could not expect to receive the payment. What if he partially cleaned his room, would I be bound to pay him? If I wrote up the agreement the way that God wrote the Law, he would merit nothing. God's obligation to reward His people depended on them obeying *all* His commandments. Any expectation for rightful blessing through the Law is dependent upon perfect obedience to the Law. And the same Scripture records how we would not perfectly obey the Law.

As if this is not clear enough, the Deuteronomy portion restates the same idea in the negative:

> "But it shall come to pass that if you will not heed the voice of the LORD your God, to observe to do all His commandments and His statutes which I command you today, then all these curses shall come upon you and overtake you." (Deuteronomy 28:15)

וְהָיָה אִם־לֹא תִשְׁמַע בְּקוֹל יְיָ אֱלֹהֶיךָ
לִשְׁמֹר לַעֲשׂוֹת אֶת־כָּל־מִצְוֹתָיו וְחֻקֹּתָיו
אֲשֶׁר אָנֹכִי מְצַוְּךָ הַיּוֹם וּבָאוּ עָלֶיךָ
כָּל־הַקְּלָלוֹת הָאֵלֶּה וְהִשִּׂיגוּךָ:

Thereafter follows 53 verses of curses.

## THE PURPOSE OF THE LAW

What happens if there is imperfect obedience, if even one commandment is disobeyed? The text seems to say that apart from doing "all" that God legislated, we are under all of the curses. However, perfect obedience is impossible. Especially since we tend to see sincere effort as "good enough," such standards can seem unfair. How does God expect anyone

23

to find blessed through an impossible standard? Doesn't He want to bless His people? This brings us to the purpose of the Law.

As mentioned, the purpose of Torah is not primarily to give laws, but to demonstrate God's character. In showing His holiness, He reveals our desperate need for His grace and mercy. His blessing is something we could never deserve. However, the Torah records how centuries before Moses, God had made an *un*conditional covenant with Abraham (Genesis 12:1-3). On the basis of the Abrahamic Covenant the Jewish people's existence, survival, and land is guaranteed. But if we ever think that such great promises demonstrate our worthiness rather than God's graciousness, God provided the Law to show what we are *really* like (Deuteronomy 9:6).

This is why in the Law itself there are provisions for our moral failure (sins). There is much material on the sacrifices for sin and the need for atonement, as in Yom Kippur, the Day of Atonement (Lev. 1—7). Even a cursory reading of the Scriptures makes it plain: the Law reveals our sinfulness and not our righteousness. The Law is like a perfect mirror, perfectly revealing our flaws. Its purpose was never to reveal how good we are or how deserving we are of God's blessing.

## THE PROMISE OF THE LAW

God's people are kept and blessed by His mercy and gracious promises. When Israel's sin of the Golden Calf deserved God's utter destruction (Exodus 32:10), Moses didn't plead for their welfare on the basis of the laws he had just delivered, but on the basis of the covenant God had made with Abraham (Exodus 32:13). The Law is the objective, holy, legal standard by which God can judge His people. Thus, through the Law, people can recognize His holiness, the evil of their sins, and absolute graciousness of His promises. The Law's holy demands upon Israel—"You shall be Holy even as the LORD your God is holy" (Leviticus 19:2)—demonstrated Israel's constant need for mercy.

The Scriptures promise what we truly needed: circumcised hearts—which only come through the New Covenant, the hope of the Torah (Deuteronomy 29:1; 30:6; Jeremiah 31:31-34). The Torah prepared God's people for the coming of His ultimate demonstration of mercy, Messiah. God's Messiah would provide final atonement for sins through His own sacrifice:

> "He was bruised for our iniquity. The LORD laid on Him the iniquity of us all. He was cut off out of the land of the living, for the transgressions of my people, to whom the judgment was due... He bore the sin of many." (Isaiah 53:5,6,8,12)

The Scriptures bring us face-to-face with a holy and yet loving God. Before Him, we all fall short. But we also see One who has mercifully provided the promise of forgiveness and life to all who will trust in His Word. Through that same grace, we are enabled to live out His grace and mercy.

Individually as Jews, and corporately as Israel, it is the gracious promise of God that is our hope. This promise is fulfilled in *Yeshua HaMashiach*, even as the New Covenant proclaims:

> "Him of whom Moses in the Law and the Prophets did write" (John 1:45).

# FOUR

# YOU MEAN, THE JEWISH SCRIPTURES TEACH ABOUT HELL?

When reading the Scriptures, one discovers that they do not attempt to prove God exists. Rather, God is presented as a reality. Just as one never has to prove the reality of parents to a child, since his own existence proves there must also be biological parents, so also, one need not prove the reality of the Creator to the creature.

Likewise, the Scriptures do not attempt to prove that Hell exists.

Yet, the absolute holiness and justice of God requires a Hell. If a person can get a life sentence without possibility of parole for evil perpetrated against a mere man, then why should it seem so strange for one to get an eternal life sentence for evil perpetrated against the Eternal God?

## THE FACT OF HELL

The psalmist writes:

> The wicked will return to Sheol, even all the nations who forget God. (Psalm 9:17[18])

יָשׁוּבוּ רְשָׁעִים לִשְׁאוֹלָה כָּל־גּוֹיִם שְׁכֵחֵי אֱלֹהִים:

> Let death come deceitfully upon them; let them go down alive to Sheol, for evil is in their dwelling, in their midst. (Psalm 55:15 [16])

יַשִּׁימָוֶת עָלֵימוֹ יֵרְדוּ שְׁאוֹל חַיִּים
כִּי־רָעוֹת בִּמְגוּרָם בְּקִרְבָּם:

The psalmist uses the word *Sheol*, the common word for Hell. Since all people die, the writer is clearly not referring to mere death or "the grave," which would be no extra punishment for the wicked. As in other texts, he must refer to a place of real punishment.

Isaiah writes:

> Nevertheless, you will be thrust down to Sheol, to the recesses of the pit. Those who see you will gaze at you, they will ponder over you saying, "Is this the man who made the world tremble, who shook kingdoms..." (Isaiah 14:15-16).

אַךְ אֶל־שְׁאוֹל תּוּרָד אֶל־יַרְכְּתֵי־בוֹר:
רֹאֶיךָ אֵלֶיךָ יַשְׁגִּיחוּ אֵלֶיךָ יִתְבּוֹנָנוּ הֲזֶה הָאִישׁ
מַרְגִּיז הָאָרֶץ מַרְעִישׁ מַמְלָכוֹת:

The prophet reveals that there is consciousness, recognition, and communication for those in *Sheol*.

The Prophet Daniel writes:

> And many of those that sleep in the dust of the ground will awake, these to everlasting life, but the others to disgrace and everlasting contempt. (Daniel 12:2)

וְרַבִּים מִיְּשֵׁנֵי אַדְמַת־עָפָר יָקִיצוּ אֵלֶּה לְחַיֵּי עוֹלָם
וְאֵלֶּה לַחֲרָפוֹת לְדִרְאוֹן עוֹלָם: ס

Daniel reveals that the final judgment that follows death is "everlasting," or *olam*. This word *olam* is also used for everlasting life. The result (*dir'on*) is disgraceful and contemptible (literally, an abhorrence).

The New Covenant is consistent with the Hebrew Scriptures regarding these same truths about Hell or Sheol, calling it "eternal fire," "eternal punishment," "the unquenchable fire," and "the penalty of eternal destruction" (Matthew 25:41, 46; Mark 9:43-48; 2 Thessalonians 1:9). We read that "it is appointed for man to die once and after this comes judgment," and that in this place, "...the smoke of their torment goes up forever and ever, and they have no rest day or night..." (Hebrews 9:27; Revelation 14:11).

This is not the Bible's attempt to frighten anyone into following God. The amount of space the Scriptures spend on Hell is little compared to that spent on the Great News about God, Messiah, love, and forgiveness. That said, the Scriptures reveal some painful facts about the hereafter.

## THE FAIRNESS OF HELL

What seems most difficult to some is what appears to be the inherent unfairness of Hell. "After all," some might say, "why would a good person have to be punished alongside of a Hitler just because he didn't follow God's way? Isn't that unfair?"

First, let us understand that no one deserves Heaven. This is God's special place and no one who sins deserves to be there (Psalm 15:1). God's standards for Heaven are high: to be with Him, you must be like Him, "Be holy as the LORD your God is holy" (Leviticus 19:2). Whoever goes to Heaven could not earn it. Their entrance into heaven is not based on what they deserve, but on the basis of God's sovereign, gracious love. Since we all have sinned, we all deserve Hell (Psalm 14:3; Isaiah 53:6). We earned it.

That said, the Scriptures teach that in Hell each gets the punishment due him. The differing degrees of punishment in Hell are determined completely on what the individual deserves. Similarly, there are differing degrees of reward in Heaven.

First, people are judged by their *deeds*:

> ...The dead, the great and the small, were standing before the throne... And the dead were judged... according to their deeds. (Revelation 20:12)

This portion teaches that if Bill and Joel were doomed to judgment, and during their lifetimes Bill embezzled ten thousand dollars, but Joel only stole one thousand, Bill's punishment may be ten times greater than Joel's punishment because his evil deeds were ten times worse. That is fair.

Second, people are judged according to their *knowledge*:

> "And the servant that knew his master's will and did not get ready or act in accord with that will, shall receive much punishment. But the one that did not know it, and committed deeds worthy of punishment, will receive little punishment. To whom much is given, much will be required." (Luke 12:47, 48)

Let us say Bill and Joel were both doomed to hell, and during their lifetimes each stole ten thousand dollars. This portion teaches that if Bill learned that it is wrong to steal and stole anyway, but Joel was not taught this truth, Bill's punishment would be greater than Joel's, because Bill knew better. He will be held more accountable for the knowledge he received. Joel still gets punished, for he still did deeds worthy of punishment, but to a lesser degree. That, too, is fair.

Finally, people are judged according to their *rank*:

> Not many of you should presume to be teachers, my brothers, because you know that we who teach will be judged more strictly. (James 3:1)

This portion teaches that different levels of responsibility can receive different levels of punishment. Bill and Joel are both guilty of embezzling ten thousand dollars each. However, if Bill was Joel's teacher (or rabbi, pastor, president), Bill's punishment may be greater than Joel's, since his position demanded a higher level of responsibility. Rank may, in some cases, have its privileges, but it certainly demands greater accountability before God.

Again, this is fair. The Scriptures teach that Hell is very fair. In Hell, tragically, people finally get what they justly deserve.

## THE FLEEING FROM HELL

> "The rich man also died and was buried. In Hell, where he was in torment… he called… 'I have five brothers… warn them, so they will not also come to this place of torment'." (Luke 16:23-27)

People might say "I want to be with my buddies in Hell," or "I want to be with my brother and father in Hell." Do you know what their buddies and family want? They want to warn everyone to flee judgment by whatever means necessary.

God cannot overlook sin, but He does love us. That's why He sent the Messiah, who died as atonement for sins, just as the Jewish prophets predicted (Isaiah 53). All who will trust in God's provision for forgiveness have new life and heaven as a gift of God. God truly desires us in Heaven, but He will not save anyone against their will. That's only fair.

# FIVE

# WHY DO WE NEED A SACRIFICE TO ATONE FOR SINS?

**M**any modern educated people tend to object to the idea of sin and sacrifice: "I don't need a sacrifice! I can just repent. I'm basically a good enough person. Besides, sin isn't all that important anyway." By contrast, people concerned with these issues (like followers of Messiah Yeshua) may seem to be either neurotically obsessed for emphasizing sin, naively barbaric for extolling sacrifice—or both!

## THE ISSUE OF SIN MINIMIZED

For most people sin and sacrifice are just not very relevant issues. Sin for the most part is viewed as a moral lapse in judgment and is atoned for with something between a sincere apology and a life sentence. The basic idea is that people are generally good, with a few obvious exceptions.

I remember handing out some Good News literature several years ago in New York City a few weeks after *Yom Kippur* (the Day of Atonement). I saw one of New York's finest, and since his Police ID revealed he was from my side of the family, I offered him a brochure. When he saw that the title spoke of the need for atonement and forgiveness, he said, "Forget it; I don't need that. The people I arrest need *that* message."

"Really," I said, "and where were you on Yom Kippur?"

"In the synagogue," he shot back, "where I was supposed to be!"

"And what did you do in the synagogue?" I asked.

"Why I was..." His voice trailed off as his fist began automatically beating his chest, as all orthodox Jews are trained to do as they repent of sins on that day.

His voice changed as he said, "Okay, I'll read one of your pamphlets." As he thought of Yom Kippur, he remembered that on the Day of Atonement, everyone must acknowledge that they have sinned. At least once a year the Torah reminds us not to be self-righteous (Lev. 23:29).

In the Prophets and the Writings, the Scriptures are perfectly clear as well regarding the sinful nature of all people:

> All we, like sheep, have gone astray; each one has turned to his own way . . . (Isaiah 53:6).
>
> כֻּלָּנוּ כַּצֹּאן תָּעִינוּ אִישׁ לְדַרְכּוֹ פָּנִינוּ
> וַיְיָ הִפְגִּיעַ בּוֹ אֵת עֲוֹן כֻּלָּנוּ׃
>
> All of us are as an unclean thing, and all our righteousness are as filthy rags (Isaiah 64:6[5]).
>
> וַנְּהִי כַטָּמֵא כֻּלָּנוּ
> וּכְבֶגֶד עִדִּים כָּל־צִדְקֹתֵינוּ

"The heart is deceitful above all things, and desperately wicked; who can know it?" (Jeremiah 17:9).

עָקֹב הַלֵּב מִכֹּל וְאָנֻשׁ הוּא מִי יֵדָעֶנּוּ:

There is none that does good, no, not one. (Psalm 14:3b)

אֵין עֹשֵׂה־טוֹב אֵין גַּם־אֶחָד:

In Your sight no man can be justified (Psalm 143:2b).

כִּי לֹא־יִצְדַּק לְפָנֶיךָ כָל־חָי:

God calls sin *wicked* and deserving of judgment, as it is rebellion and disobedience to Him. For a person to label sin as unimportant doesn't make it any less wicked, just as changing the label on a bottle of rat poison to read "fruit juice" doesn't make the contents any less deadly. In fact, now it becomes even more dangerous, since someone may think that taking a drink could actually be nutritious!

If this seems like an overstatement, understand that the Scriptures reveal just how disastrous sin is. According to the Prophet Ezekiel said:

"The soul that sins, it shall die!" (Ezekiel 18:4b).

הַנֶּפֶשׁ הַחֹטֵאת הִיא תָמוּת:

This is the eternal judgment that is also spoken of by Daniel the Prophet. We previously considered this time when eternal judgment will be dispensed:

"Those who sleep in the dust of the earth will awake, some to everlasting life and some to everlasting contempt" (Daniel 12:2).

וְרַבִּים מִיְּשֵׁנֵי אַדְמַת־עָפָר יָקִיצוּ
אֵלֶּה לְחַיֵּי עוֹלָם וְאֵלֶּה לַחֲרָפוֹת לְדִרְאוֹן עוֹלָם:

35

Isaiah reveals that though people think they pray and are heard by God, their sins actually break that prayer connection:

> ... the LORD's hand is not so short that it cannot save; nor is His ear so dull that it cannot hear. But your iniquities have made a separation between you and your God, and your sins have hidden His face from you so that He does not hear. (Isaiah 59:1-2)

הֵן לֹא־קָצְרָה יַד־יְיָ מֵהוֹשִׁיעַ
וְלֹא־כָבְדָה אָזְנוֹ מִשְּׁמוֹעַ׃
כִּי אִם־עֲוֺנֹתֵיכֶם הָיוּ מַבְדִּלִים בֵּינֵכֶם לְבֵין אֱלֹהֵיכֶם
וְחַטֹּאותֵיכֶם הִסְתִּירוּ פָנִים מִכֶּם מִשְּׁמוֹעַ׃

## GOD'S WAY OF ATONEMENT

People discuss whether the Temple, which was a place of sacrifices, will ever be rebuilt in Jerusalem. The problem with rebuilding the Temple is not simply a Muslim mosque atop the Temple Mount, as tradition has taught that we do not need *blood atonement* for sins. Yet the Scriptures state that blood sacrifice is *necessary* to atone for sins:

> "The life of the flesh is in the blood; and I have given it to you upon the altar to make atonement for your souls; for it is the blood that makes atonement for the soul" (Leviticus 17:11).

כִּי נֶפֶשׁ הַבָּשָׂר בַּדָּם הִוא וַאֲנִי נְתַתִּיו לָכֶם עַל־הַמִּזְבֵּחַ
לְכַפֵּר עַל־נַפְשֹׁתֵיכֶם כִּי־הַדָּם הוּא בַּנֶּפֶשׁ יְכַפֵּר׃

In fact, Yom Kippur is truly a day of atonement only if the atonement is made God's way-- by blood sacrifice (Leviticus 16). Acknowledging and repenting of one's sins is essential, but by itself this is like attempting to dismiss a murder charge by apologizing to the offended party. Sin is horrific to God, and He is the offended party.

Biblical Jewish faith takes *teshuvah* (repentance) along with blood sacrifice as both essential for atonement. The reality of blood sacrifice can seem bizarre or primitive, but it teaches us the real horror of sin: it kills.

Rather than needing to be explained away, the sacrifices function like promissory notes which are paid off by Yeshua. The sacrificial system illustrates the final, perfect sacrifice that God Himself provided in the Messiah:

> "Surely He has borne our griefs and carried our sorrows; yet we esteemed Him stricken and afflicted by God... But he was wounded for our transgressions, he was bruised for our iniquities... the Lord has laid on Him the iniquity of us all... He was cut off from the land of the living for the transgression of my people was He stricken... He shall make His soul an offering for sin... My righteous Servant shall justify the many, for He shall bear their iniquities . . . He bore the sin of many and made intercession for the transgressors." (Isaiah 53:3-12, selections)

This chapter shows how God would provide for our sins through Messiah's atonement. The prophet begins the chapter by asking, *"Who has believed our report?" (Isaiah 53:1)*. That's still the question today: Who will believe God, His view of sin, and His way of forgiveness?

The New Covenant provides what the Hebrew Scriptures predicted: *"God demonstrates His own love toward us, in that while we were yet sinners, Messiah died for us" (Romans 5:8)*. All who trust in Messiah Yeshua for their atonement receive forgiveness for their sins, and best of all, an eternal relationship with God!

## SIX

# HOW CAN A MAN BECOME GOD?

Sometimes humor can best illustrate how a Biblical idea is misunderstood. An Irish Catholic named John and his Jewish friend Saul were talking about how John's son Patrick had just been made a priest.

"So what's the big deal about that, John?" Saul asked.

"It's a very big deal, Saul. As a priest he can one day become a bishop!" John responded.

"So what's the big deal about that?"

"Saul, as a bishop, Patty can one day become a cardinal. Imagine, my son, the Cardinal!" John was getting excited now.

"*Nu*," Saul said, "what's the big deal about that?"

"Saul, my friend, as Cardinal, Patty could be... Oh, be still my heart... he could become Pope!"

Saul again asked, "what's the big deal?"

Now impatient, John demanded, "what do you expect, for him to become God?!!"

Triumphantly, Saul said, "and why not, one of *our* boys made it!"

The mistaken notion is that Yeshua, a man, became God. This is *not* the message of the Scriptures. The Scriptures are quite clear on this point: no man can become a god. However, on the other hand we know that *"nothing is impossible for God!"* (Genesis 18:14; Luke 1:37). The Hebrew Scriptures prophesy and the New Covenant declares that in Yeshua, God Himself, *Adonai*, became a man—He took on human flesh.

Three questions raised on this issue help us consider it more fully:

1) Can God come in the flesh?

2) Was Messiah expected to be God?

3) Did the New Covenant declare Him as such?

## CAN GOD COME IN THE FLESH?

To find the answer let's look at the visitation to Abraham in the book of Genesis, chapter 18. The passage begins, *the LORD appeared to him by the Oaks of Mamre. (Genesis 18:1)*

$$\text{וַיֵּרָא אֵלָיו יְיָ בְּאֵלֹנֵי מַמְרֵא}$$

The next verse states that *as he lifted his eyes, three men stood by him.* Abraham and Sarah then prepared food for these guests (18:3-8). Was it merely a vision? Impossible, for not only do you not prepare food for a vision, but visions don't eat, and these men did (Genesis 18:8).

Now, two of these three men are later identified as angels (compare Genesis 18:22 and 19:1). However, the third, who ate (v.8), spoke (v.10), and walked with Abraham (v.16, 22), is identified as "the LORD" Himself. In Genesis 18:13, the text states, *And the LORD said to Abraham...*

$$\text{וַיֹּאמֶר יְיָ אֶל־אַבְרָהָם}$$

The word translated *the LORD* throughout this portion is called the Tetragrammaton—the four Hebrew letters that make up the sacred Name of God (*yud, hey, vav,* and *hey,* rendered in the Hebrew selections above with two *yud's*, as is customary to show respect).

Do the Hebrew Scriptures teach that God came in the flesh? Clearly, the answer is yes!

## WAS MESSIAH EXPECTED TO BE GOD INCARNATE?

However, what was the Biblical expectation for the Messiah? Was he to be God incarnate? The Prophets, especially Isaiah and Micah, most directly answer this. Isaiah wrote:

> For a child shall be born to us and a son shall be given; and the government shall be upon His shoulder; and His name shall be called: Wonderful Counselor, Mighty God, Everlasting Father, Prince of Peace (Isaiah 9:6 [5]).

$$\text{כִּי־יֶלֶד יֻלַּד־לָנוּ בֵּן נִתַּן־לָנוּ}$$
$$\text{וַתְּהִי הַמִּשְׂרָה עַל־שִׁכְמוֹ}$$
$$\text{וַיִּקְרָא שְׁמוֹ פֶּלֶא יוֹעֵץ אֵל גִּבּוֹר}$$
$$\text{אֲבִיעַד שַׂר־שָׁלוֹם:}$$

This is traditionally recognized as referring to Messiah: "I have yet to raise up the Messiah, of whom it is written, *for*

41

*a child is born to us [Isaiah 9:5]*" (Deuteronomy Rabbah 1.20).

Isaiah predicts that one coming from the *Galilee* will bring *light, joy* and *victorious peace* because He is the *Prince of Peace (Sar Shalom)*, and indeed, the *Mighty God (El Gibbor,* Isaiah 9:1-5). This child to be born is the theme of Isaiah 7:12, where it states He would be born of a *virgin* (7:14). He is *the root of David* that *Gentiles will trust in* (11:10), as well *the remnant of Israel* (10:20-23).

The truth of who this One will be is reiterated when the Scripture says that not every Jewish person will believe, but only a remnant: *the remnant shall return, the remnant of Jacob, to the Mighty God [El Gibbor]* (Isaiah 10:21).

שְׁאָר יָשׁוּב שְׁאָר יַעֲקֹב אֶל־אֵל גִּבּוֹר׃

Micah the prophet gives further detail about Messiah's Divine Nature, and specifically from where He would come:

> But you, Bethlehem Ephratah, little among the thousands of Judah, out of you will go forth for Me, One who will be ruler in Israel, whose goings forth have been from days of eternity." (Micah 5:2 [1])

וְאַתָּה בֵּית־לֶחֶם אֶפְרָתָה
צָעִיר לִהְיוֹת בְּאַלְפֵי יְהוּדָה
מִמְּךָ לִי יֵצֵא לִהְיוֹת מוֹשֵׁל בְּיִשְׂרָאֵל
וּמוֹצָאֹתָיו מִקֶּדֶם מִימֵי עוֹלָם׃

Micah clearly states that Israel's ruler would not only come from *Bethlehem*, but his *goings forth* would be from *eternity*. That is, He who would be born in Bethlehem is God, the Eternal One! Thus the Messiah—the One to bring peace, joy and life to all who would believe (the remnant); the One who would be born in Bethlehem, yet live in Galilee—this One is the Lord, the Mighty God Himself!

## Does the New Covenant proclaim Yeshua as Messiah and God?

Hundreds of times the New Covenant unequivocally declares Yeshua to be the Messiah. (The word "Christ" is a transliteration, not a translation, of the Greek word *christos,* translated correctly into English as "Messiah" or "anointed one.")

His Deity is indicated repeatedly by His title "Lord" and His identification as *the* Lord of the Hebrew Scriptures. Please note that when referring to Yeshua, the New Covenant repeatedly uses portions of the Tanakh that actually refer to God (Mark 1:1-3, Heb. 1:8-12).

The New Covenant writers were clear regarding Messiah's Divine nature:

> In the beginning was the Word, the Word was with God, the Word was God . . . and the Word became flesh and dwelt among us (John 1:1,14).

Mostly, Yeshua's divinity was assumed, and written about in order to make an application for our lives:

> Each of you should not look merely to your own interests but also to the interests of others. Your attitude should be the same as that of Messiah, who being in very nature God, did not consider equality with God something to be grasped, but humbled Himself, taking on the form of a servant, coming in human appearance. . . Being found in human form, He humbled Himself and became obedient unto death, even death by the cross (Philippians 2:4-8).

What amazing love is demonstrated in the humility of our Messiah! The One who is the Eternal God, *Adonai*, came in the flesh to die for our sins and conquer death, that anyone might have forgiveness, life, joy and peace by trusting in Him. No man can become a god, but in accordance with the Scriptures, God Himself took on human flesh, in the person of Yeshua, the Messiah of Israel.

# SEVEN

# IF THE MESSIAH HAS ALREADY COME, THEN WHY ISN'T THERE PEACE?

The story goes something like this: A person considering whether Yeshua could be the promised Messiah, asks his rabbi, "Could it be that Messiah has come and that Yeshua is His name?" The rabbi walks over to the window, looks out, shakes his head and with a sigh exclaims: "He can't be the true Messiah. There's still no peace. We know that when Messiah comes there will be peace everywhere."

Isn't it true that Messiah is to bring peace? And if Yeshua is the Messiah, then… *where's the peace?*

## THE PROMISE OF PEACE

The desire for peace is universal among the sane nations of this world. However, the biblical idea of peace means much more than merely the end of political hostilities. The

Hebrew word "shalom" has in it the idea of completeness or wholeness. Because of sin, we all are incomplete. The Scriptures tell us that sin separates us from God, from each other, and even from ourselves. The "Shalom of God" fulfills us perfectly and completely.

The Scriptures present this as the very desire of God, who in Aaron's blessing states, *"May the Lord give you peace"* (Numbers 6:26); the Psalmist writes *"The Lord will bless His people with peace"* (Psalm 29:11); and in the Prophets, Messiah is even called *"Prince of Peace"* (Isaiah 9:6). In fact, when Messiah reigns, peace will be His Kingdom's theme (Isaiah 2:1-4; 9:4-5,7; Zechariah 9:9-10).

This universal peace of Messiah is based first on everyone having personal peace through a right relationship with God:

> "You will keep him in perfect peace whose mind is steadfast, because he trusts in You" (Isaiah 26:3).

יֵצֶר סָמוּךְ תִּצֹּר שָׁלוֹם שָׁלוֹם כִּי בְךָ בָּטוּחַ:

Thus when each person receives peace from God, each one can share and live in that peace within their family, community, country and world. It's like wanting to give a million dollars to a friend, but if you don't have it, you can't give it. You can't give what you don't have.

## THE REJECTION OF PEACE

The Scriptures prophesy that when God's peace would be offered, but the offer would be turned down. In fact, Isaiah the Prophet wrote that Messiah, the Prince of Peace, would come to make peace between God and His people, but that He Himself would be "despised and rejected by men." Why would Messiah be rejected?

"He had no beauty or majesty to attract us to Him, nothing in His appearance that we should be attracted to Him" (Isaiah 53:2).

For people attracted to externals, Messiah would be too ordinary looking. There was nothing about His appearance to command our attention. For those who were looking, it was not His external appearance, but His internal character that made Him stand out.

"He was a man of sorrows and familiar with suffering. Surely, He took upon Himself our griefs and sorrows, yet we considered Him stricken by God and afflicted by Him" (Isaiah 53:3-4).

For people desirous of comfort and convenience, this One suffered too much. How could someone suffer so much at the hands of religious people and the government, and not be judged by God? In any case, no decent person would want to associate with someone who attracted trouble the way this one did.

The truth is, however, He suffered for our sins, and not His own: *"The Lord laid on Him the iniquity of us all"* (Isaiah 53:6).

"He was brought as a lamb to the slaughter, as a sheep before the shearers is silent, so He did not open His mouth" (Isaiah 53:7).

He seemed too compliant, too passive. He wasn't exactly a John Wayne or Arnold Schwarzenegger type of warrior king. Many wanted a messiah who would come and vanquish the enemies of Israel, and thus create a forced peace. His humility was despised and rejected, for He came not to protect His own life, but to be an offering for our sins: *"the Lord makes His life a guilt offering"* (Isaiah 53:10).

Now suppose I came to your house with a beautiful cake (my father always taught me not to show up empty handed when visiting), but as soon as you saw me you slammed the door in my face! Would you still expect to get the cake? Of course not! Reject me, and you reject all that I bring with me. So, why isn't there peace? When Messiah, the Prince of Peace, is rejected, then His peace is rejected as well.

## THE PROVISION OF PEACE

The New Covenant Scriptures repeat the promise of Isaiah 26:3 (mentioned above). All who will trust in Messiah and the atonement that He made for sins, receives

1) Peace with God

2) Peace of mind and heart

3) Peace with one another

> 1) "Therefore, having been made right with God by faith, we have peace with God through our Lord Yeshua the Messiah" (Romans 5:1).

> 2) "The peace of God, which is beyond all understanding, will guard your hearts and minds in Messiah Yeshua" (Philippians 4:7).

> 3) "For He is our peace, who has made both (Jews and Gentiles) ... into one new man, thus establishing peace" (Ephesians 2:14,15).

The Scriptures also teach that one day our people, Israel, will acknowledge the Messiah and receive His salvation and peace: *"The stone which the builders rejected shall become the capstone!"* (Psalm 118:22-26). In light of that event, we are commanded to *"Pray for the peace of Jerusalem"* (Psalms 122:6). In that day, in the Messiah, peace will be worldwide, even as the Scriptures promise.

## A Picture of Things to Come

A illustration of this future peace comes from a friend of mine, a Jewish man named Joel* serving in the Israeli army. In his unit he was known as "the believer," due to his outspoken faith in Messiah. He was back on reserve duty in Gaza, patrolling the streets and alleyways after curfew. It was a moonlit night and they felt rather exposed. They came upon a van parked in a suspicious place, and realized it could be booby trapped. The squad leader, remembering that Joel had so much "faith," had him investigate.

Joel cautiously approached the van, as the soldiers looked on from a safe distance. Suddenly a nearby doorway opened to an apartment building and an Palestinian Arab walked out.

"Halt," he commanded, his gun raised. "What are you doing here?"

"I am pastor and I am visiting people from my church," the man replied.

Joel proceeded to interrogate the man on the spot.

"So do you believe Yeshua died for sins?"

The pastor said, "yes."

"Do you believe he was raised bodily from the dead?"

"Yes, I do."

"Do you believe that He is going to return, and reign in Jerusalem?"

Later on, the pastor said that he felt like was having flashbacks to his time before the ordination board.

* Names changed for privacy

Still, he looked at Joel and said, "with all my heart I wait for the return of our Savior."

At this point Joel had put his rifle to his side. "If what you say is true, then you are my brother in the Lord, because I too believe that Yeshua is our Messiah." They were hugged and laughed in fellowship in the Gaza moonlight.

When Joel returned to his squad, their eyes were like saucers. As the shock wore off they asked, "what on earth were you doing with that Palestinian?"

"That man is my brother in the Messiah, and Messiah is the hope for our people."

# EIGHT

# DO YOU REALLY EXPECT ME TO BELIEVE IN THREE GODS?

There is no one like God. Yet, a common misconception about the faith of New Covenant believers is that we teach "belief in three gods." For many, this summarizes the issue of the Trinity. However, clear teachings in the New Covenant prove otherwise:

> And Yeshua answered him and said, "The first of all the commandments is: Hear O Israel, the Lord our God is one Lord" (Mark 12:29; 1 Corinthians 8:4; James 2:19).

New Covenant faith is monotheistic; the word "Trinity" itself is a contraction of "Tri-unity," emphasizing that God is One. But, sadly, confusion prevails because of general ignorance about what is often called "God's mystery nature." Learning about these things is not only important so that faith in Messiah might be better communicated to

51

those who do not yet believe, but that believers themselves might relate to what the Bible says in a Jewish frame of reference. In other words, believers need to understand that the Tri-unity of God is not a gentile fable or *goyisha bubbemeises*, but revealed truth.

## "ONE" WORDS

The testimony of the Jewish Scriptures is the authority for knowing about God, and as we look into Torah specifically we see the basis of the Unity of God presented: *"Hear O Israel, the Lord is our God, the Lord is one"* (Deuteronomy 6:4).

*Sh'ma Yisrael, Adonai Eloheinu, Adonai echad*

שְׁמַע יִשְׂרָאֵל יְיָ אֱלֹהֵינוּ יְיָ אֶחָד:

One Jewish man commented to me, "God is mentioned three times right there in the verse that speaks of His oneness!" Yes, but for now let us notice that the word "one" (*echad*, in the original Hebrew) can point to a oneness-in-plurality. For example, when God established the marriage relationship, the Scripture states:

> For this cause a man shall leave his father and mother and cleave to his wife; and the two shall be <u>one</u> flesh (Genesis 2:24).

עַל־כֵּן יַעֲזָב־אִישׁ אֶת־אָבִיו וְאֶת־אִמּוֹ
וְדָבַק בְּאִשְׁתּוֹ וְהָיוּ לְבָשָׂר אֶחָד:

Here we see that this word for "one" (*echad*) is not used to indicate something utterly singular, but a oneness-in-plurality. Numbers 13:23 likewise uses the same word to speak of one cluster of grapes. And a cluster has a plurality of grapes!

If the Scriptures had wanted to describe God as one in the singular sense with no possibility of a triune nature, there is another word for one in the Hebrew, *yachid.* For instance, *yachid* is used when God was speaking to Abraham about Isaac: *"Take now your son, your <u>only</u> son" (Genesis 22:2).*

קַח־נָא אֶת־בִּנְךָ אֶת־יְחִידְךָ

Although Abraham had another son, Ishmael, God refers to Isaac as a one-of-a-kind son, the son of the covenant (this language prefigures Messiah as shown in Hebrews 11:17; John 3:16).

*Yachid* is used twelve times in the Hebrew Scriptures, and speaks of a unique or lone oneness (Genesis 22:2, 12, 16; Judges 11:34; Jeremiah 6:26; Amos 8:10; Zechariah 12:10; Psalm 22:20[21]; 25:16; 35:17; 68:6[7]; Proverbs 4:3). However, the word *yachid* is never used regarding God! In light of the rampant polytheism (worship of many gods) in the ancient world, *yachid* would have been useful if the Scriptures were to deny the notion of there being more than one person who is God. *Yachid* is *never* used in the Bible to describe the Divine nature, and to use it in that way would have been to deny the reality of the triune nature of God.

## TRADITION OR TRUTH?

There is a place where *yachid* is used to describe God-- in the Thirteen Principles of Faith written by the great medieval sage Maimonides (*Rambam*). He wrote the second of the thirteen principles specifically to deny the triune nature of God. It reads:

> I believe with perfect faith that the Creator, blessed be His name, is a Unity (yachid), and that there is no unity in any manner like unto His, and that He alone is our God, who was, is, and will be.

We agree that the Creator is a Unity; in fact, there is no other unity like His; indeed, God alone is Eternal.

Yet it is interesting that the word used for God's Unity here is *yachid*. Prior to Maimonides, the word *echad* was always used when referring to God's Unity. As the polemical conflict between Rabbinic Judaism and hostile anti-Jewish Christendom worsened, the rabbis' concept of God became defined increasingly in contrast to Christian teaching. Sadly, down to our own day this conflict has led to deep misunderstanding of what the Scriptures themselves teach. However, the biblical view of God's nature has been preserved by a remnant of the Jewish community— Jewish followers of Yeshua.

This nature of God is often presupposed in the Scripture, not explained. That is why we come across interesting portion like the following in Genesis:

> The LORD rained upon Sodom brimstone and fire from the LORD out of heaven (Genesis 19:24).

וַיְיָ הִמְטִיר עַל־סְדֹם וְעַל־עֲמֹרָה גָּפְרִית
מֵאֵת יְיָ מִן־הַשָּׁמָיִם׃

The Lord was on the earth raining down fire and brimstone, also coming from the Lord out of heaven. The Hebrew text presents Him as if there are *two distinct persons,* in *two places at once!*

Even from the first verse of Genesis, it is interesting that the word used for God, *Elohim,* has a plural ending. When God created man, we are brought into the counsels of God's own heart:

> And God said, "Let Us make man in Our image, according to Our likeness" (Genesis 1:26).

וַיֹּאמֶר אֱלֹהִים נַעֲשֶׂה אָדָם בְּצַלְמֵנוּ כִּדְמוּתֵנוּ

Notice the plural possessive pronoun "Our." Various theories have been given for such language. Yet the passage does not indicate that He was speaking to angels, as it goes on to say:

> So God created man in His own image, in the image of God He created him; male and female He created them (Genesis 1:27).

וַיִּבְרָ֨א אֱלֹהִ֤ים ׀ אֶת־הָֽאָדָם֙ בְּצַלְמ֔וֹ
בְּצֶ֥לֶם אֱלֹהִ֖ים בָּרָ֣א אֹת֑וֹ
זָכָ֥ר וּנְקֵבָ֖ה בָּרָ֥א אֹתָֽם׃

HaShem alone is the Creator, not a group of "angelic artists," and it is HaShem's image in whom we have been created, not the images of angels.

Furthermore, the idea that God is declaring a "plurality of majesty" while suitable for Elizabethan England, does not work for the Ancient Near East. In the Bible, no king is referred to using the plurality of majesty. The best explanation is that the plural pronouns point to a mystery which is internal to God's own nature.

Isaiah the Prophet also assumes this nature of God in several places. In the vision of his own commission as a prophet of Israel, Isaiah writes:

> Also I heard the voice of the Lord, saying, "Who will go for Us, whom shall We send?" (Isaiah 6:8).

וָאֶשְׁמַ֞ע אֶת־ק֤וֹל אֲדֹנָי֙ אֹמֵ֔ר
אֶת־מִ֥י אֶשְׁלַ֖ח וּמִ֣י יֵֽלֶךְ־לָ֑נוּ
וָאֹמַ֖ר הִנְנִ֥י שְׁלָחֵֽנִי׃

Once more in God's own counsel, God refers to Himself with a <u>plural</u> pronoun. Isaiah again assumes this unity-in-plurality of God's Nature when he refers to the practical activity of God concerning our redemption:

> "Come near to Me, hear this: I have not spoken in secret from the beginning; from the time it was, there am I; now the Lord GOD and His Spirit has sent Me" (Isaiah 48:16).

קִרְבוּ אֵלַי שִׁמְעוּ־זֹאת לֹא מֵרֹאשׁ בַּסֵּתֶר
מֵעֵת הֱיוֹתָהּ שָׁם אָנִי
וְעַתָּה אֲדֹנָי יְיָ שְׁלָחַנִי וְרוּחוֹ׃

God alone is from the beginning, even as it says in Genesis 1:1, "in the beginning God created Heaven and earth." Earlier in the 48th chapter of Isaiah, the Lord says this:

> "I have declared the former things from the beginning; they went forth from My mouth, and I caused them to hear it. Suddenly I did them, and they came to pass. ... Before it came to pass I proclaimed it to you, so that you would not say, 'My idol has done them, and My graven image and my molten image have commanded them.'" (Isaiah 48:3, 5).

הָרִאשֹׁנוֹת מֵאָז הִגַּדְתִּי
וּמִפִּי יָצְאוּ וְאַשְׁמִיעֵם
פִּתְאֹם עָשִׂיתִי וַתָּבֹאנָה׃
וָאַגִּיד לְךָ מֵאָז בְּטֶרֶם תָּבוֹא
פֶּן־תֹּאמַר עָצְבִּי עָשָׂם
וּפִסְלִי וְנִסְכִּי צִוָּם׃

Thus in Isaiah 48:16, it is the Lord Himself ("Me") who is sent by the Lord God and His Spirit! Many more portions of the Jewish Scriptures address the same truth: There is only One God. Yet this one God is revealed in three Persons: Father (Isaiah 63:16; 64:8), Son (Isaiah 9:5[6]; Proverbs 30:4), and the Holy Spirit (Isaiah 48:16; 63:10; or the Spirit of God, Isaiah 63:14).

In light of the many polytheistic religions surrounding Israel at that time, the Tanakh emphasized the oneness of God, while remaining faithful to the subtle teaching of His mystery nature. The New Covenant now progressively reveals more of this tri-unity (as in Matthew 28:19, "… immersing them in the name of the Father, the Son, and the Holy Spirit…"), while still being faithful to the truth that there is only one God.

The New Covenant reveals the truth of God's triune nature, not to imply that there is more than one god, but to be faithful to the revelation of God's nature as seen in Tanakh. The Tri-unity is not a contradiction of the oneness of God, but the best explanation of His oneness.

## SO WHAT?

Admittedly, understanding these matters can be difficult, but God's triune nature is better appreciated if we see its application for our lives. To know the triune God is to know One who is eternally relational. The Father, the Son, and the Holy Spirit are fully God, and in community with one another. The Eternal God is love, because Father, Son, and Holy Spirit are in eternal fellowship together. Thus Yeshua can say, *"By this all men will know that you are My disciples, if you have love for one another" (John 13:35).*

We read from Genesis 1:27 that God made us in His image: "male and female He created them." God created us for relationship with Him and with each other. Since relationship is intrinsic to the triune God, it is intrinsic to our lives as well.

Trusting in this matter also shows us our finite limitations, as shown in this story of the theologian Augustine. He was walking along a beach, trying to understand the Tri-unity. As he struggled in thought ("three in one, one in three... *Oy vey!*"), he saw a young boy digging a hole in the seashore and then run back to the ocean over and over taking water from the ocean and pouring it in the hole. Augustine asked him, "Child, what are you doing?"

The boy said, "I'm just trying to put the ocean in this hole!"

Augustine laughed and said to himself, "that's what I was trying to do, too!"

Mysteries are not like problems to be solved, but rather places where we should fall down to worship. Rather than believe only what we can comprehend, we have faith in God's testimony:

> "Trust in the LORD with all of your heart, and do not lean on your own understanding" (Proverbs 3:5).

בְּטַח אֶל־יְיָ בְּכָל־לִבֶּךָ וְאֶל־בִּינָתְךָ אַל־תִּשָּׁעֵן׃

> "For My thoughts are not your thoughts. For as the heaven is higher than the earth, so My thoughts are higher than your thoughts" (Isaiah 55:8-9).

כִּי לֹא מַחְשְׁבוֹתַי מַחְשְׁבוֹתֵיכֶם
וְלֹא דַרְכֵיכֶם דְּרָכָי נְאֻם יְיָ׃
כִּי־גָבְהוּ שָׁמַיִם מֵאָרֶץ
כֵּן גָּבְהוּ דְרָכַי מִדַּרְכֵיכֶם
וּמַחְשְׁבֹתַי מִמַּחְשְׁבֹתֵיכֶם׃

In the end, our faith rests on trusting the testimony of Scripture as the true revelation of God; regarding both His nature, and His method of reconciling sinful people to Himself; His free gift of forgiving sins through the atonement in Messiah Yeshua!

# NINE

# ISN'T A VIRGIN BIRTH ... INCONCEIVABLE?

O f all the miracles the Bible attributes to God, it seems the Virgin Birth of Messiah arouses the most controversy. But the same Bible that reveals God declares the virgin birth to be a historical fact. Some question whether it can be considered a scientific fact since it can not be observed nor repeated. But then what miracle can be? The Virgin Birth is yet another unique and miraculous work of the God of Israel!

## AN ISSUE OF MIRACLES

Miracles may be irrelevant for those that dismiss the possibility of God. But if God is even a possibility, then so are miracles. "But still," you might think, "the virgin birth is hard to believe." Actually, it depends on *how big* your God is! For the One who is the Creator of all, no miracle is too difficult, and thus, no miracle should be dismissed out of hand.

## CHAPTER NINE

Also, for Jews, miracles are the *only rationale* for our own existence. After all, if left to the preferences of the Egyptians and Pharaoh, the Persians and Haman, or the Nazis and Hitler, we wouldn't be here at all! Yet while other ancient peoples have come and gone (do you know any Hittites?), the Jewish people remain. God promised to keep us as a people, and miraculously He has done it.

## MIRACLE BIRTHS ARE JEWISH!

Moreover, miraculous *births* are a big part of our particular history. When God decided to bless the world through a people whom He loved and by whom the Messiah would come (Genesis 12:3), God chose Abraham and Sarah. As the Scriptures teach us, Abraham was too old, and Sarah was barren (Genesis 11:30). Thus we have a problem: God purposely chose to make a nation from the one couple that couldn't have kids!

Rather than being a problem for God, such human limitations made the *point*. As the promise of God would effectively bless the world, so also it would take the power of God to make it happen. And miracle of miracles, Isaac was born.

Isaac then married Rebecca. She too was barren, but again God intervened (Genesis 25:21). And again with Jacob and Rachel, who was barren (Genesis 29:31). God miraculously provided a miracle birth (Genesis 30:22-24).

To recap, biblical history shows that the existence of the Jewish people is based upon miracle births from God. Rather than seeming abnormal, a miracle birth for the Jewish Messiah should be part of our expectations for Him. After all, shouldn't we expect the most unusual person in the universe to have a most unusual entrance in His birth? His unique nature would actually require it!

## PROPHECY OF A VIRGIN BIRTH

The Scriptures create an expectation for the Virgin Birth, as this same hope is seen in the first messianic prophecy:

> "And I will put enmity between thee (Satan) and the woman, and between thy seed and her seed; it shall bruise thy head, and thou shalt bruise his heel" (Genesis 3:15).

וְאֵיבָה אָשִׁית בֵּינְךָ וּבֵין הָאִשָּׁה
וּבֵין זַרְעֲךָ וּבֵין זַרְעָהּ
הוּא יְשׁוּפְךָ רֹאשׁ וְאַתָּה תְּשׁוּפֶנּוּ עָקֵב׃

God promised to remove that Serpent of old, Satan, the father of lies and anti-Semitism, through a redeemer who would come from the 'seed' of the woman. This is God's first attention-getting clue: a woman would be the instrument of Messiah's coming.

In the prophet Isaiah we read Messiah's prophetic birth announcement to the House of David:

> "The Lord himself shall give you a sign: Behold, the virgin shall conceive and bear a son, and shall call His name Immanuel" (Isaiah 7:14).

לָכֵן יִתֵּן אֲדֹנָי הוּא לָכֶם אוֹת
הִנֵּה הָעַלְמָה הָרָה וְיֹלֶדֶת בֵּן
וְקָרָאת שְׁמוֹ עִמָּנוּ אֵל׃

Some object against the word 'virgin' as an accurate translation of the Hebrew word *almah*. Yet in the Hebrew Scriptures, the word *almah* is used seven times (Genesis 24:43; Exodus 2:8; Proverbs 30:18; Psalm 68:25; Song of Solomon 1:3; 6:8), and every time it speaks of young women who have not had sexual relations.

In the 2nd and 1st centuries BCE, the Hebrew Scriptures were for the first time translated into Greek. According to tradition, it was done by seventy rabbis, and this accounts for its name *Septuagint* (LXX), meaning 70. They translated *almah* as *parthenos,* or "virgin." This was centuries before Messiah and rightly used by the New Covenant (Matthew 1:23). So, there are no good grounds thinking 'virgin' is an inaccurate or biased reading of the Isaiah text.

It is sometimes argued that a different Hebrew word, *betulah*, would have served as a closer word for 'virgin'. However, the two Hebrew words are largely synonymous (cf. Gen. 24, where Rebekah is identified by both), and therefore either would make the point. In fact, it is not clear whether *betulah* would actually have been a good choice, since it is also used for a widow in Joel 1:8.

## WHAT'S IN A NAME?

But, why the name "Immanuel" in Isaiah 7 rather than "Yeshua"? Many places in the Hebrew Scriptures tell us about Messiah, each giving us different names. Thus, in Isaiah 9:5(6), He is called "Wonderful Counselor, Mighty God, Eternal Father, Prince Of Peace," and in Jeremiah 23:6, He is called "the LORD our Righteousness." Unlike modern names, each of these describes some quality of God's nature or character.

*Immanu El* (two words) means "God is with us." God will neither leave nor forsake us in our sins, for Messiah, the hope of the House of David, has come. Faith in Messiah brings eternal relationship with God, for in Messiah Yeshua "God is with us!"

Isaiah told wicked King Ahaz that "if you will not believe you not will be established" (Isaiah 7:9). The same is true for each of us. Let us have faith in the God of Israel's greatest miracle, Messiah, that we may be eternally established before Him.

# TEN

# HOW CAN YESHUA POSSIBLY BE THE SON OF DAVID?

S ome say that the Virgin Birth means Yeshua* cannot be the Messiah. You see, one of the necessary credentials of the true Messiah of Israel is that He be from the line of King David (Isaiah 7:13-14; 9:7[6]; Jeremiah 23:5-6). Since Yeshua did not have an earthly father, and it would be this lineage which goes back to David, it is thought that Yeshua could not be of the line of David. In other words, if He was born of a virgin, wouldn't this disqualify him from being "the son of David"?

## A TALE OF TWO LINEAGES

Yet in fact, Yeshua's Davidic line goes not only through his stepfather, Joseph, but also through His mother Miriam. Luke's account traces Miriam's genealogical line back to King David:

63

> Now Yeshua Himself began His ministry at about thirty
> years of age, being (as was supposed) the son of Joseph,
> the son of Heli, the son of Matthat, the son of Levi
> ... the son of Rhesa, the son of Zerubbabel, the son of
> Shealtiel, ... the son of Nathan, the son of David, the
> son of Jesse (Luke 3:23-31).

Scholarship has uncovered interesting things about this
genealogy. Descent through the father's side was vital in
the first century. The Talmud makes it clear that "only the
father's family is called family; the mother's family is not
called family" (Yevamot 54b). So when Luke gives Miriam's
lineage, he follows the officially authorized and expected
route by attaching it to his step-dad, Joseph.

On the Greek phrase "as was supposed," Risto Santala writes,
"The Greek phrase corresponds to the Hebrew expression
*ke-hozqâ* or *kemô huhzaq*, which means that the matter had
been legally confirmed. Thus, before the law, it was right to
connect Yeshua through Joseph to his father-in-law," that
is, Miriam's father - "Heli," or Eli. *(The Messiah in the New
Testament in the Light of Rabbinical Writings, tr. William
Kinnaird, Jerusalem: Keren Ahvah Meshihit).*

On the other hand, Matthew records that genealogical line
of Joseph himself goes back to King David:

> ... David the king begot Solomon... Josiah became
> the father of Jeconiah... Shealtiel begot Zerubbabel.
> Zerubbabel begot Abiud, ... Eleazar begot Matthan,
> and Matthan begot Jacob. And Jacob begot Joseph the
> husband of Miriam, of who was born Yeshua who is
> called Messiah (Matthew 1:6-16, selections).

Reading "begot" in the most natural way—that is, taking
it to refer to biological descent—indicates that Matthew

records Joseph's genealogy. Thus we have two distinct lineages presented in the two Good News accounts. Joseph came through David's most famous son, Solomon; and Miriam through Nathan, another son of David.

Hence, the two accounts tell us that Joseph and Miriam are both from the lineage of King David. But there is more to the story, since the Tanakh gives some relevant clues as to why Yeshua's unique lineage matters.

## Curse of Jeconiah?

According to the prophet Jeremiah, Jeconiah (a descendant of King David), had come under a curse and made David's seed through Jeconiah invalid to serve as King:

> Thus says the LORD, "Write this man down childless, a man who will not prosper in his days; for no man of his descendants will prosper sitting on the throne of David or ruling again in Judah" (Jer. 22:30).

כֹּה ׀ אָמַר יְיָ כִּתְבוּ אֶת־הָאִישׁ הַזֶּה עֲרִירִי
גֶּבֶר לֹא־יִצְלַח בְּיָמָיו
כִּי לֹא יִצְלַח מִזַּרְעוֹ אִישׁ יֹשֵׁב
עַל־כִּסֵּא דָוִד וּמֹשֵׁל עוֹד בִּיהוּדָה:

Since Joseph was from that line, no physical son of Joseph could inherit the throne of David. Miriam's line, though, was untainted, thus her son could legitimately lay claim to the Davidic throne.

However, as a stepfather, Joseph was Yeshua's legal guardian. Thus Joseph provides a legal tie to the line of David for Yeshua. Thus, Joseph's genealogy is relevant for Matthew's record. It shows that Yeshua had no father or guardian from outside the line of David that would give Him a non-Davidic lineage.

On the other hand, even if only His mother was in the line of David, it would still be sufficient for Yeshua to be of Davidic lineage. Some might protest that the mother's side cannot give genealogical credentials, and it is true that the biblical records are patrilineal. However, in the Scriptures there are clear exceptions regarding the right of a female to pass along the family heritage (Numbers 27:1-7).

So, whether viewed from the stepfather's legal side, or from the mother's biological side, Yeshua is "the son of David," and the authorized Messiah of Israel. In fact, since the Messiah was prophesied to be "virgin-born" (Isaiah 7:13-14), this is the very way the lineage would have had to have been worked out.

The fact that the true Messiah not only had to be a son of David, but virgin-born as well, narrows down the field quite a bit. Other than Yeshua, what legitimate claimants are there for the position?

## DAVID'S SON, DAVID'S LORD

Paradoxically, Messiah the son of David was also to be the Son of God—in fact, Messiah was actually to be Mighty God (Isaiah 9:6[5], in Hebrew, *El Gibbor*). The son of David was not only to reign from David's throne over all Israel, but to have ultimate authority over all of the peoples of the world (Isaiah 2:1-4; 11:10; 49:6). Yeshua is the only claimant with the proper credentials. David wrote:

> Kiss the Son, lest He be angry, and ye perish in the way,
> For His wrath will soon be kindled. Blessed are all they
> that take refuge in Him. (Psalm 2:12)

נַשְּׁקוּ־בַר פֶּן־יֶאֱנַף ׀ וְתֹאבְדוּ דֶרֶךְ
כִּי־יִבְעַר כִּמְעַט אַפּוֹ
אַשְׁרֵי כָּל־חוֹסֵי בוֹ׃

In this messianic psalm, "Kiss the Son" means to give homage to the King, as is symbolized by kissing His ring. King Messiah is the One who has authentic authority over each of our lives. He is the true Son of God to whom homage is due. Yeshua is the one and only Son of David who can give true security to our people for today, and for eternity, even as was prophesied in Jeremiah 23:5-6:

> "Behold, the days are coming," says the LORD, "that I will raise up for David a righteous Branch; a King shall reign and prosper, and execute judgment and righteousness in the earth. In His days Judah will be saved, and Israel will dwell securely. And this is His name by which He will be called: 'The LORD our Righteousness'."

הִנֵּה יָמִים בָּאִים נְאֻם־יְיָ
וַהֲקִמֹתִי לְדָוִד צֶמַח צַדִּיק
וּמָלַךְ מֶלֶךְ וְהִשְׂכִּיל
וְעָשָׂה מִשְׁפָּט וּצְדָקָה בָּאָרֶץ׃
בְּיָמָיו תִּוָּשַׁע יְהוּדָה
וְיִשְׂרָאֵל יִשְׁכֹּן לָבֶטַח
וְזֶה־שְּׁמוֹ אֲשֶׁר־יִקְרְאוֹ יְיָ ׀ צִדְקֵנוּ׃

One day Israel as a people will enjoy this security when we as a nation return to the son of David, Messiah Yeshua the Lord, even as prophesied in Hosea 3:5:

> "Afterward the children of Israel shall return and seek the LORD their God and David their King. They shall fear the LORD and His goodness in the latter days."

אַחַר יָשֻׁבוּ בְּנֵי יִשְׂרָאֵל
וּבִקְשׁוּ אֶת־יְיָ אֱלֹהֵיהֶם וְאֵת דָּוִד מַלְכָּם
וּפָחֲדוּ אֶל־יְיָ וְאֶל־טוּבוֹ בְּאַחֲרִית הַיָּמִים׃

Today as individuals, anyone can return to the true Lord and King, Yeshua, and be saved, dwell securely and receive His goodness. Let us "give homage to the Son" by yielding to His authority through obedience to His Word. As we acknowledge our sins and depend on His atonement, trusting in His sacrifice, we can rest knowing He is the Lord our Righteousness.

# ELEVEN

# WHY WOULD THE JEWISH MESSIAH HAVE TO COME TWICE?

To some it appears that followers of Yeshua are in denial of the painful truth by believing in "the Second Coming." "Why would it be necessary for Messiah to come twice," the doubtful ask. "Didn't he get it right the first time? And, if he is the Jewish Messiah, as you claim, where in the Jewish Scriptures does it say anything about two comings of the Messiah?"

## Two Pictures of the Messiah

The issue of "two comings" of the Messiah is neither non-Jewish nor particularly unusual to Jewish thought. For two millennia the rabbinical community has been discussing, pondering and conjecturing the possible ways to resolve paradoxical and seemingly contradictory references to the Messiah in the Jewish Scriptures.

On one hand, the Scriptures present a picture of the Messiah reigning:

> "The kings of the earth take their stand against the LORD and His Messiah. The LORD laughs at them saying, `I have installed My King on Zion'" (Psalm 2:2, 4)

> יִתְיַצְּבוּ ׀ מַלְכֵי־אֶרֶץ וְרוֹזְנִים נוֹסְדוּ־יָחַד
> עַל־יְיָ וְעַל־מְשִׁיחֽוֹ :
> יוֹשֵׁב בַּשָּׁמַיִם יִשְׂחָק אֲדֹנָי יִלְעַג־לָֽמוֹ :

> "Behold, days are coming," says the LORD, "that I will raise up for David a righteous Branch, and a King shall reign and prosper" (Jeremiah 23:5).

> הִנֵּה יָמִים בָּאִים נְאֻם־יְיָ
> וַהֲקִמֹתִי לְדָוִד צֶמַח צַדִּיק
> וּמָלַךְ מֶלֶךְ וְהִשְׂכִּיל

In these portions, and in many others (Genesis 49:10; Numbers 24:17; Psalm 45:6-7; Ps. 110:1-7; Isaiah 2:1-4; 11:10; Zechariah 14:3-4, 16), Messiah is pictured as ruling and reigning over the enemies of God. This is a time of peace and joy, where Israel is the chief of the nations again, and the Davidic throne is gloriously established in Jerusalem.

However, alongside this exalted scene, there is also the picture of Messiah being rejected and forsaken:

> "And the Messiah will be cut off and will have nothing" (Daniel 9:26).

> "He had no beauty or majesty to attract us to Him, nothing in His appearance that we should be attracted to Him. He was a man of sorrows and familiar with suffering. Surely, He took upon Himself our griefs and

sorrows, yet we considered Him stricken by God and afflicted by Him. We did not esteem Him. Who of His generation considered Him? For He was cut off from the land of the living for the transgressions of my people to whom the stroke was due" (Isaiah 53:2-8).

"I am a worm and not a man, scorned by men and despised by the people... All who see me mock me and hurl insults... You lay me in the dust of death... They have pierced my hands and my feet." (Psalm 22:6, 7, 15, 16 [7, 8, 16, 17]).

וְאָנֹכִי תוֹלַעַת וְלֹא־אִישׁ חֶרְפַּת אָדָם וּבְזוּי עָם׃
כָּל־רֹאַי יַלְעִגוּ לִי׃
וְלַעֲפַר־מָוֶת תִּשְׁפְּתֵנִי׃
כָּאֲרִי יָדַי וְרַגְלָי׃

In these portions and many others (Isaiah 49:7; 50:6; Psalm 69:4-22; Zechariah 11:12) Messiah is seen as rejected and suffering in innocence for the sins of others. Therefore, two different works of Messiah are presented in Scripture:

1) He will suffer and die for sins

2) He will reign and rule in peace

## TRADITIONAL THEORIES

These two contrasting pictures of the biblical Messiah have brought about various theories of how the Messiah could both reign, and yet be rejected; a celebrated victor, while also a sacrificial victim. Rabbinical explanations have included: a Resurrected Messiah; a Leper Messiah; a Beggar Messiah; and even Two Messiahs—Messiah *Son of Joseph*, who would innocently suffer as the Patriarch Joseph suffered, and Messiah *Son of David*, who will reign as David reigned. These ideas are quite prevalent in the

71

rabbinical literature (Sukkot 52a,b; Gen. Rabbah LXXV, 6; XCV; XCIX, 2; S.S. Rabbah II, 4; Num. Rabbah XIV, 1; Sefer Sippurim Noraim 9a-b, 10b). Within all these theories, we see traditional Jewish scholarship debating the best harmonization of these two contrasting pictures of the biblical Messiah.

## TWO COMINGS REVEALED

Hosea the Prophet speaks to the subject as well, as he presents God speaking to a wayward Israel:

> "Then I will go back to My place until they admit their guilt and seek my face; in their misery they will earnestly seek Me" (Hosea 5:15).

אֵלֵךְ אָשׁוּבָה אֶל־מְקוֹמִי
עַד אֲשֶׁר־יֶאְשְׁמוּ וּבִקְשׁוּ פָנָי
בַּצַּר לָהֶם יְשַׁחֲרֻנְנִי ׃

We see God offended at Israel's sins and going *back to [His] place (Heaven) until they admit guilt.* The implication is that *when* they *admit their guilt, then* He will return to them. This is clearly stated in Israel's response to the Lord's departure from them:

> "Let us acknowledge the LORD; let us press on to acknowledge Him. As surely as the sun rises, He will appear; He will come to us like the winter rains, like the spring rains that water the earth" (Hosea 6:3).

וְנֵדְעָה נִרְדְּפָה לָדַעַת אֶת־יְיָ
כְּשַׁחַר נָכוֹן מוֹצָאוֹ וְיָבוֹא כַגֶּשֶׁם לָנוּ
כְּמַלְקוֹשׁ יוֹרֶה אָרֶץ ׃

Though God had left, they had confidence He would also certainly return. In the Lord's statement there was hope that their admission of guilt would bring about His return.

In light of all this discussion it should surprise no one that the Messiah Himself would come and clarify these apparently contradictory pictures of His work. Similar to the portion in Hosea, Yeshua says to Israel:

> "You shall not see me again until you say 'Blessed is He that comes in the name of the Lord'" (Matthew 23:39).

Following Yeshua's death, burial, resurrection and ascension ("back to My place"), Peter proclaims in Jerusalem:

> "Repent, then, and turn to God, so that your sins may be wiped away, that the times of refreshing may come from the Lord, and that He may send the Messiah, who has been appointed for you, even Yeshua. He must remain in Heaven until the time comes for God to restore everything, as He promised long ago in the holy prophets." (Acts 3:19-21)

Though the return of the Messiah is mentioned many times in the New Covenant (Matthew 24-25; 1 Thessalonians 1:10; 4:13-5:9; Revelation 22, etc.), this revelation regarding the two works of Messiah is not an innovation. Rather, it is a clear fulfillment of what the Jewish Scriptures prophesied: Messiah would come to die for our sins, be raised from the dead, go back to His place, and return as we acknowledge our guilt and call out to Him. Just as Joseph was at first rejected by his brothers, then later accepted (Genesis 37, 50), and as Moses was first rejected by Israel, then later accepted (Exodus 2:14, 4:31), so Messiah would be rejected and then later accepted by Israel:

> "They will look unto Me (God) whom they have pierced, and mourn for Him as one mourns for an only son" (Zechariah 12:10b).

וְהִבִּיטוּ אֵלַי אֵת אֲשֶׁר־דָּקָרוּ
וְסָפְדוּ עָלָיו כְּמִסְפֵּד עַל־הַיָּחִיד
וְהָמֵר עָלָיו כְּהָמֵר עַל־הַבְּכוֹר׃

The Jewish Scriptures are to be fulfilled *in every detail.* Just as the Jewish Messiah described in the Scriptures had to suffer and die for sins, so He will also return to reign and bring peace.

# TWELVE

# IF YESHUA IS THE JEWISH MESSIAH, THEN WHY DON'T MOST JEWS BELIEVE IN HIM?

Many find it rather strange that the Jewish Messiah could have come, and comparatively so few Jews believe it. Occasionally, the question sounds something like this: *"With all the scholars and rabbis searching to discover the Messiah, how is it that you're the only genius to figure this out?"*

Actually, the number of Jewish people today who believe in Yeshua ranges somewhere between 200,000 to over a million, a number including both scholars and laymen. However, this number (which depends on how one counts children of intermarried, etc.), while significant, is still nowhere near the majority of Jewish people.

Some may believe that the truth is determined by a majority vote. While this plays a role in the politics of men, it has nothing to do with the truth of God.

## CHAPTER TWELVE

In the Hebrew Scriptures, the prophet Isaiah declares that most Jewish people would not recognize the Messiah when He would initially come:

> Who has believed our report? To whom has the arm of the Lord been revealed?
>
> For He grew up before Him as a tender shoot, as a root out of dry ground; He would have no majesty that would attract us, nor any beauty that we would desire Him.
>
> He was despised and forsaken of men, a man of sorrows, and acquainted with grief, and we hid as it were our faces from Him; He was despised and we esteemed Him not (Isaiah 53:1-3).

God knew and revealed to Isaiah what may not seem all that hard to figure out: Most people don't want God's way of salvation—even religious people! In fact, that's exactly what Isaiah goes on to say:

> All we like sheep have gone astray, each one has turned to his own way; but the LORD has laid on Him the iniquity of us all (Isaiah 53:6).

Though the true Messiah would be our sin-bearer, when He first came He would *not* be accepted but rejected by the majority of the Jewish people. Isaiah makes this matter crystal clear by further stating:

> A remnant shall return, even the remnant of Jacob to the Mighty God (Isaiah 10:21; see also Isaiah 9:6[5]).

שְׁאָר יָשׁוּב שְׁאָר יַעֲקֹב אֶל־אֵל גִּבּוֹר:

We recognize then that a "remnant" (שְׁאָר), a small portion of the whole nation, would believe and make *teshuvah* (repentance). Only this remnant would "return to the

Mighty God." This is a prediction fulfilled in the Jewish people who have come to believe in Yeshua. Similarly, the New Covenant discusses and compares the present situation of the Jewish people with their condition in the time of Elijah the prophet:

> Even so, then, at this present time also there is a remnant according to the election of grace (Romans 11:5).

Though the Scriptures make it clear, some will still wonder how the majority of rabbis could have "missed it." The answer is that the Messiah who God promised and sent was not the Messiah the world or most rabbis were looking for. They wanted a Messiah who would forcibly remove Roman domination over Israel, and return Israel to its former glory. Our agenda does not always match up with God's.

In God's eyes, our true problem is not external, but internal. It is ultimately not a matter of having the right information, but a matter of the heart (Jeremiah 17:9). The power of sin corrupts the souls of all men and women, whether Jewish or non-Jewish.

Thus to satisfy God's justice, and spare mankind the punishment we deserve, the purpose of Messiah's first coming was to die for sins. And rather than approve all of the traditional judgments of the rabbis, He insisted that the religious leaders of Israel would have to repent as well! This was intolerable for the majority of the religious leadership, and Messiah was rejected.

Therefore, even though many accepted Yeshua as the Messiah, the majority of Jewish people and rabbis did not respond favorably to Him, just as predicted.

However, the Prophets also predict there will come a time when our people will *nationally* come to believe in Him:

"I will pour upon the house of David and the inhabitants of Jerusalem the Spirit of grace and supplication; and they shall look on Me whom they have pierced, and mourn for Him as one mourns for an only son" (Zechariah 12:10).

וְשָׁפַכְתִּי עַל־בֵּית דָּוִיד
וְעַל יוֹשֵׁב יְרוּשָׁלַ͏ִם רוּחַ חֵן וְתַחֲנוּנִים
וְהִבִּיטוּ אֵלַי אֵת אֲשֶׁר־דָּקָרוּ
וְסָפְדוּ עָלָיו כְּמִסְפֵּד עַל־הַיָּחִיד
וְהָמֵר עָלָיו כְּהָמֵר עַל־הַבְּכוֹר׃

"The stone which the builders rejected shall become the chief of the corner!" (Psalms 118:22)

אֶבֶן מָאֲסוּ הַבּוֹנִים הָיְתָה לְרֹאשׁ פִּנָּה׃

Which brings us to today. Though one day, our people as a nation will trust in Yeshua as their Messiah and King, even now there is a "remnant of Israel" who believes in the Messiah. This remnant acknowledges Yeshua for what the Hebrew Scriptures and New Covenant declare Him to be: the Messiah and Savior of our people, and all people.

## THIRTEEN

# AREN'T CHRISTIANS AND THE NEW TESTAMENT ANTI-SEMITIC?

Because Jewish history is filled with persecution by many so-called Christians, it is easy to presume that the New Testament is guilty until proven innocent. "Isn't the New Testament anti-Semitic? Doesn't it teach Christians to hate Jews? What about Christian anti-Semitism and the Holocaust?" These are certainly valid questions, but to some, the facts regarding the Scriptures may be quite surprising.

### THE NEW TESTAMENT IS JEWISH?

It's a shock to many people when they discover just how *Jewish* the New Testament actually is. Jeremiah the prophet foretold that God would give the New Testament (or New Covenant, *Brit Chadashah* in Hebrew) to our people:

> "Behold, the days are coming when I will make a New
> Covenant with the House of Israel and with the House

of Judah, not like the covenant that I made with your fathers in the day I took them by the hand to bring them out of the land of Egypt, a covenant which they broke, though I was a husband to them," says the LORD.

"For this is the covenant I will make with the house of Israel, after those days," declares the LORD. "I will put My Law within them and I will write it on their hearts, and I will be their God and they shall be My people."

"And they will not teach each one his neighbor, and each man his brother, saying, 'Know the LORD', for they will all know Me, from the least to the greatest of them," says the LORD.

"For I will forgive their iniquities and remember their sins no more." (Jeremiah 31:31- 34[30-33])

הִנֵּה יָמִים בָּאִים נְאֻם־יְיָ
וְכָרַתִּי אֶת־בֵּית יִשְׂרָאֵל
וְאֶת־בֵּית יְהוּדָה בְּרִית חֲדָשָׁה:
לֹא כַבְּרִית אֲשֶׁר כָּרַתִּי אֶת־אֲבוֹתָם
בְּיוֹם הֶחֱזִיקִי בְיָדָם
לְהוֹצִיאָם מֵאֶרֶץ מִצְרָיִם
אֲשֶׁר־הֵמָּה הֵפֵרוּ אֶת־בְּרִיתִי
וְאָנֹכִי בָּעַלְתִּי בָם נְאֻם־יְיָ:
יְ זֹאת הַבְּרִית אֲשֶׁר אֶכְרֹת
אֶת־בֵּית יִשְׂרָאֵל
אַחֲרֵי הַיָּמִים הָהֵם נְאֻם־יְיָ
נָתַתִּי אֶת־תּוֹרָתִי בְּקִרְבָּם
וְעַל־לִבָּם אֶכְתֲּבֶנָּה
וְהָיִיתִי לָהֶם לֵאלֹהִים

וְהֵמָּה יִהְיוּ־לִי לְעָם:
וְלֹא יְלַמְּדוּ עוֹד אִישׁ אֶת־רֵעֵהוּ
וְאִישׁ אֶת־אָחִיו לֵאמֹר דְּעוּ אֶת־יְיָ
כִּי־כוּלָּם יֵדְעוּ אוֹתִי
לְמִקְטַנָּם וְעַד־גְּדוֹלָם נְאֻם־יְיָ
כִּי אֶסְלַח לַעֲוֺנָם
וּלְחַטָּאתָם לֹא אֶזְכָּר־עוֹד:

The New Covenant is what Messiah Yeshua initiated when He died to make atonement for sins. It is His death that established the basis of the New Covenant relationship between God and His people: the forgiveness of sins for all who will believe.

From my experiences among Christians growing up in New York, I assumed that the New Testament was a combination religious rulebook for Gentiles and instruction manual for anti-Semitism. Upon reading it for myself, I was surprised to find that the New Covenant is actually the Lord's love letter to those who seek Him.

## TRUE YESHUA FOLLOWERS LOVE THE JEWS

As far as being a cause for anti-Semitism, this could never happen for those who have read its pages and believed its words. In the pages of the New Testament, Yeshua is presented as "the King of the Jews." He is shown weeping over Jerusalem (Luke 19:41), expounding the Law and the prophets (Matthew 5:17), and identifying primarily with the Jewish people in His daily activities (Matthew 10:5,6; 15:24).

How could any follower of Yeshua claim to have the King of *the Jews* in their hearts, and yet hate the Jewish people? Absurd! Rather, true Gentile followers of the Jewish Messiah

81

love the Jewish people. The life and teachings of Yeshua give no justification for any kind of hatred, let alone hatred of His Jewish people, *"for the love of Messiah controls us"* (2 Corinthian 5:14).

Therefore, it is better said that *anti-Semitism is proof of the ignorance of those who disobey Messiah and His teachings.*

The experience of the Holocaust of the 1930's and 40's, as well as other anti-Semitic persecutions, are often thought of as an expression of Christian hatred toward the Jewish people. After all, the members of the Nazi party were all baptized as infants into the state church. However, Nazi ideology was anti-Christian as well as anti-Jewish, and in reality, many governments have abused religion in an attempt to justify their pragmatic, national interests.

The Hebrew Scriptures reveal the truth that *Anti-Semitism is anti-God.* This is revealed by the Psalmist:

> O God, do not remain quiet; Do not be silent and, O God, do not be still.
>
> For behold, Your enemies make an uproar, and those who hate You have exalted themselves.
>
> They make shrewd plans against Your people, and conspire together against Your treasured ones.
>
> They have said, "Come, and let us wipe them out as a nation, That the name of Israel be remembered no more."
>
> For they have conspired together with one mind; against You they make a covenant. (Psalm 83:1-5 [2-6])

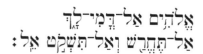

אֱלֹהִים אַל־דֳּמִי־לָךְ
אַל־תֶּחֱרַשׁ וְאַל־תִּשְׁקֹט אֵל׃

כִּי־הִנֵּה אוֹיְבֶיךָ יֶהֱמָיוּן
וּמְשַׂנְאֶיךָ נָשְׂאוּ רֹאשׁ:
עַל־עַמְּךָ יַעֲרִימוּ סוֹד
וְיִתְיָעֲצוּ עַל־צְפוּנֶיךָ:
אָמְרוּ לְכוּ וְנַכְחִידֵם מִגּוֹי
וְלֹא־יִזָּכֵר שֵׁם־יִשְׂרָאֵל עוֹד:
כִּי נוֹעֲצוּ לֵב יַחְדָּו
עָלֶיךָ בְּרִית יִכְרֹתוּ:

True Gentile followers of Messiah were persecuted, imprisoned and murdered by the Nazis for helping the Jews in their areas. Jewish believers in Messiah were killed as quickly as the other Jews. There was nothing about the vicious hatred toward the Jewish people that represented anything taught in the New Covenant, or by faithful followers of Messiah Yeshua.

## THE CAUSE OF ANTI-SEMITISM

The New Covenant teaches us how the Jewish Messiah came to resolve a problem that is universal: the problem of sin. Sin, the power that spurred the Nazis is essentially the same problem *all* people have—rebellion against God. This sin problem ends when a person, any person, acknowledges their sin to God, and places their trust in Messiah Yeshua.

I once had the opportunity to speak at a businessmen's breakfast where I shared the message of Yeshua. I invited the people there to respond to God's love and forgiveness in the Jewish Messiah. Of those who responded, I remember one businessman who burst into tears. Up to that point he had been an anti-Semite, but now he was convinced of his sinfulness and wanted to repent. After we prayed he mentioned that he was stunned to have heard the message of forgiveness and new life in the *Jewish* Messiah from a *Jewish* man! It became clear to him that his baseless hatred was just one symptom of his rebellion to God—affirming the scriptural truth that anti-Semitism is anti-God, and anti-Messiah.

As evil and offensive as anti-Semitism is, all sin is offensive to God. Though some sins are not nearly so blatant, God is aware of them all. All who sin need to repent in order to be forgiven and find healing. The message of Good News is for all who will trust in Israel's Messiah and the Savior of the world, Yeshua.

# FOURTEEN

# WHY THE HOLOCAUST?

Upon seeing the name "Bialystok," I cried. Perhaps part of it was from the previous two hours I had experienced at the Holocaust Museum in Washington, D.C. My mother and her immediate family, the Hirshbeins, moved to the U.S. from Bialystok, Poland before Hitler's invasion. Those who escaped survived; the rest of the family perished as the Nazis eradicated the Jewish community of Bialystok.

The Holocaust was not the first atrocity in history, and sadly, the prophets indicate that it won't be the last. The Jewish prophet Zechariah predicted an even more horrible period for our people. Whereas about one third of Jewish people in the world were murdered under the Nazis, Zechariah prophesies that two thirds of the Jewish people will be lost in a future tribulation (Zech. 13:8).

Why, God, why? *Why the Holocaust?*

## THE ENEMY OF GOD

Evil exists because of our free choice, which includes the freedom to love or rebel against God. God will ultimately defeat evil, but currently anti-Semitism is a special kind of evil. The Scriptures are clear that the basis of this specific evil of anti-Semitism is *spiritual warfare.*

The Scriptures inform us that there is an enemy of God, *HaSatan* (Hebrew for "the adversary"). The Adversary is working to defeat and dethrone God (Isaiah 14:12-14), as impotent, futile, and laughable such a task may seem.

## THE ENEMY'S STRATEGY

God cannot lie (Titus 1:2). The Adversary's plan is to prove God wrong by nullifying God's promises made to the Jewish people through the Jewish Messiah. God has promised that the Jewish people would always survive as a people (Jeremiah 31:35-37), and would also be the conduit of the Messiah, the savior of the world.

Satan is trying to remove the Jews as a people, and his strategy is two-fold:

1. *Stop the Jews from living!* The Psalms describe this most obvious strategy:

> "Your foes rear their heads.... They plot against those You cherish ."Come," they say, "let us destroy them as a nation, that the name of Israel will be remembered no more" (Psalm 83:1-5).

Simply put: if you destroy the Jews then you prove God is a liar. For if God can't keep His people as He promised, then no one can trust any of His promises. Additionally, if

Satan can destroy Israel as a people, he proves himself to be greater than God!

The Hamans, Herods, and Hitlers were instrumental in the plan of *HaSatan*. However, that they are tools of Satan in no way excuses their culpability. We all are responsible for our actions, regardless of who or what influences us in those actions. Nevertheless, destruction of the Jews has been an important strategic goal of the enemy.

2. *Stop the Jews from living as Jews!* The second, more subtle (though potentially just as effective) strategy is to make Jewish identity repugnant, or at least irrelevant, to Jewish people themselves. In this way, Jewish people would not want to remain Jewish, and Israel would cease to be an identifiable nation before God.

In the book of Esther, we read of Mordecai's bad advice which Esther followed: "Don't reveal you're a Jew" (Esther 2:10). Only when she changed course from that counsel and revealed her Jewish identity was catastrophe averted.

This same bad advice has been relived by many of our people in every generation; in an attempt to fit into the Hellenistic culture of early second century BCE, some Jews actually had their circumcision surgically reversed! Even today, being Jewish is often so poorly understood that many make no attempt to maintain their heritage.

The shame of it all is that there are some Jewish believers in Yeshua* who do not maintain their Jewish identity. In some cases they didn't value their Jewishness before they came to faith in Yeshua. For others, it's because they are told that as followers of Yeshua they are no longer Jews. In any case, by not identifying as Jews they play right into Satan's plan: stop the Jewish people from existing as an identifiable

---

people. In so doing, we not only make discredit our faith among the general Jewish community, but we work against the very testimony of God's faithfulness (Jeremiah 31:36).

Though he was an apostle to the Gentiles, Paul understood what was at stake: the very faithfulness of God. Would the Good News of Yeshua that Paul proclaimed to Gentiles mean that God had rejected His people? His answer:

> "By no means! For I am an Israelite, a descendant of Abraham, from the tribe of Benjamin. God will not reject his people He foreknew" (Romans 11:1-2).

Every Jewish believer who states "I am an Israelite" or "I am a Jew" (Acts 22:3)—as opposed to "I was a Jew" or "I am a former Jew"—confirms that God keeps His people. God is faithful, and Yeshua is the hope of Israel, not their destroyer!

## THE ENEMY'S DESTROYER

Therefore for the sake of testifying of God's faithfulness in light of this trenchant spiritual warfare, Jewish believers have a responsibility to maintain Jewish identity. In this responsibility, there will be flexibility and variation as to how we express our Jewishness, just as the larger Jewish community enjoys its liberty in the various expressions of Jewish identity. However, our lives must in some way declare *"Am Yisrael Chai b'Yeshua HaMashiach* - the People of Israel live in Yeshua the Messiah!"

God promised that the Redeemer of mankind and the Destroyer of Satan would be the Messiah of Israel (Gen. 3:15).

To prevent his own demise Satan would need to stop this Redeemer from coming and fulfilling His mission. We see how this dovetails with his previous ploy, since the Redeemer was promised to come through the Jewish people (Genesis 12:3; 22:18; 49:10; Isa.11:10; 49:5-7).

## AM YISRAEL CHAI !

It seems that Satan has failed on this point, since Messiah has come. But if so, then why is there still anti-Semitism today after Messiah's resurrection?

The survival of the Jewish people is the linchpin of God's future activity and victory, because the return of the Lord is tied to the repentance of Israel. Yeshua said to our people:

> "You will not see me again until you say, *Baruch Haba B'Shem Adonai*, 'Blessed is He that comes in the Name of the Lord'" (Matthew 23:39).

Just as David could not rule over all of Israel and remove the adversaries until the people accepted him as king (2 Samuel 5:1-5), Yeshua will not return to reign on the Davidic throne and remove the adversary, Satan, until the Jewish people acknowledge Him as King.

Peter reiterates this point when he proclaims to the Jewish people:

> "Repent and turn to God, that your sins might be wiped away, in order that the times of refreshing might come from the Lord, and that He might send the Messiah, who has been appointed for you - even Yeshua. He must remain in Heaven until the time comes for God to restore everything, as He promised..." (Acts 3:19-21).

The return of Yeshua will "restore everything" and bring "the times of refreshing." Messiah's reign on earth is tied to the Jewish people "repenting and returning to God." Therefore, Satan is desperately trying to avoid his own demise by preventing the return of Messiah. He is doing all he can do to destroy Israel and the Jewish people now; at the same time he is trying to make faith in Yeshua so alien and repugnant that no self-respecting Jew, let alone the nation, would ever desire to repent and turn to Yeshua!

Horrors of this magnitude occur because of satanic spiritual warfare, ultimately directed against Messiah Himself. Congregations of believers in Yeshua, Jewish or Gentile, who do not endeavor to bring the Good News to the Jewish people play into Satan's plot to prevent Israel from recognizing their Messiah. It is incumbent not only to remember the Holocaust and "pray for the peace of Jerusalem" (Psalm 122:6), but believers should do all they can to bring the Good News of Messiah to the Jewish people around the world.

## FIFTEEN

# WHAT IS THE JEWISH WAY TO GOD?

The God of Israel desires to provide people with His rest and peace through an eternal relationship with Himself. Let us review five biblical realities taken from the Prophet Isaiah, which will help us to recognize that how we can have that relationship. Just as believers have often used a series of verses from Romans called the "Romans Road," we can call this "Isaiah Avenue."

### SINNERS BEFORE GOD

> All of us have become like a one who is unclean, and all our righteous acts are like filthy rags; we all shrivel up like a leaf, and like the wind our sins sweep us away (Isaiah 64:6[5]).

We may judge ourselves by *relative* standards, thinking "I'm as good as the next person" or, "I'm no worse than the next guy." Yet God judges each of us by *absolute* standards of Himself and His Law: *"You shall be holy as the Lord your God is holy"* (Leviticus 19:2). By His standards, we are all moral failures.

Granted, you may be a nice person, and you may remember to call your mom on Mother's Day; its just that you and 'the next person' still fall short of God's standards. By the way, every rabbi, priest and minister has the same problem. Psalm 14:3 declares, "there is none that does good, no not one." So, no one can point fingers or throw stones at anyone else; we all have the same great problem.

## SEPARATION FROM GOD

> Surely the arm of the Lord is not too short to save, nor His ear too dull to hear. But your iniquities have separated you from your God; your sins have hidden His face from you so that He will not hear (Isaiah 59:1,2).

The result of our sins is a broken relationship with God. Now you may pray and even fast, but the Scripture is clear: *He will not hear.*

Imagine that I steal money from you, and then have the *chutzpah* (nerve) to come to and ask you for a gift! Your response should be, "first let's deal with the past offense, then we can consider your present or future needs." God wants to bless you, but your sins separate you from Him, and must be dealt with first before He can bless you.

If this separation continues to our death, it becomes a judgment of everlasting separation from God. This breaks God's heart. He truly loves you and desires you to have everlasting life with Him. That's why the story doesn't end here, but continues on with Good News for your life.

## SALVATION IN GOD

All we like sheep have gone astray, each of us have turned
to his own way; but the Lord has laid on Him [Messiah]
the sins of us all (Isaiah 53:6).

God has provided the way of salvation and forgiveness,
since we can do no deed to save ourselves. Because of his
great love, he has promised to send Messiah to die as the
atonement or payment for our sins.

In the New Covenant, Messiah Yeshua (Jesus) states as well,
"I give my life as a ransom for many" (Matthew 20:28).
This is the salvation and right relationship that God freely
offers.

## THE SAVIOR IS GOD

To us a child is born, to us a son is given, and the
government shall be upon His shoulders. And His name
shall be called Wonderful Counselor, Mighty God,
Everlasting Father, Prince of Peace (Isaiah 9:6[5]).

Only God Himself could provide the perfect sacrifice
for sins, as He alone is perfect. What amazing love and
humility, that the Mighty God of Israel would be born,
live as a man, and die as our perfect atonement. Messiah
Yeshua is *Adonai*, the Lord.

## STAYED UPON GOD

"You will keep in perfect peace him whose mind is
steadfast, because he trusts in You" (Isaiah 26:3).

Perfect peace (*shalom shalom*) is found only in God and is
accessible only through trust in Messiah. Simple but sincere
acknowledgement of sins and trust in Messiah Yeshua as
our saving atonement is all that God requires.

Faith (trust) is necessary for a true relationship with God. The Scripture says: *"Abraham believed God, and He credited it to him as righteousness" (Gen. 15:6).* Like Abraham, you can have a right relationship with God by faith in what He alone has provided, and by obeying God in that trust relationship you will grow in His love and life. Here's a simple prayer that can assist you:

> "Lord, please forgive me for all my sins through Messiah's atonement. Help me to follow Yeshua and honor You. Thank you for loving me. Amen."

# JEWISH STORIES OF FAITH

# Life in the Shadow of the Swastika

by Frieda Roos

I was born and raised in Amsterdam, Holland, of Jewish parents. They never talked about God, and I had never been in a synagogue except for my brother's wedding. For me, Yom Kippur meant a day off from school, and the only Jewish events that took place in our home were the Bar-Mitzvahs of my two brothers! Still, we considered ourselves very Jewish. In my teenage years I had a Gentile boyfriend, and since my parents had forbidden me from seeing him because he was a Gentile, we often sneaked into a local Catholic church to be together. I was always impressed by the paintings there of the crucifixion and moved by the sadness expressed in the face of Jesus, as the artist perceived the magnitude of that event. But the times were soon to change: I would become a fugitive, running for my very life.

## From Singer to Survivor

The Lord blessed me with a soprano singing voice, and after a time studying at the Amsterdam Conservatory, I embarked on a career that would lead me to sing the Dutch version of Disney's Snow White. From there my work included: the Grand Diploma in the Geneva World Contest; the role of the Forestbird in Wagner's Siegfried with the Bayreuth Festspielhaus; a performance of Verdi's Requiem for the Queen of Holland; many live broadcasts and concert performances; and oratorios like Handel's "The Messiah" and the many beautiful Christian cantatas by Bach.

But, when the Second World War began, my singing career ended abruptly. I was immediately disqualified from any and all regular concert performances because I was Jewish.

The newspaper reviews read, "this soloist is not worth reviewing, after all the suffering brought upon us by the Jews." The Germans did allow a temporary Jewish theater, so I became involved in performing with German Jewish refugee artists for the Jewish population.

Meanwhile, the Nazis brought to another theater on the next block, Jews that they had rounded up for deportations to the infamous concentration camps. Because of my involvement with the Jewish Council, who sponsored our work in the theater, we were allowed to minister to the thousands of deportees and were guaranteed we would be the last ones to go.

The 'deportation theater' was a madhouse of anguish and filth, housing up to 9,000 people in a place built to seat 1,000. Sick people, old and young, crying children, were huddled together in fear of death, sleeping on louse-infested mattresses all over the floor. There were only two toilet facilities. I contracted lice and scabies all over my body, so much so, that when an opportunity did present itself for me to go into hiding, I couldn't because of my condition.

While at the theater I became good friends with Henny. Her husband had been arrested by the Gestapo, and we decided that I would stay in her house and help with her two small children. My former boyfriend, unbeknownst to me, had become a Gestapo agent out of anger against my parents. Not only did he try to destroy the Jewish people, but he sent the storm troopers after me at Henny's place. They came at night, fired shots through the house, but failed to find us: we hid in a heavy steel dumbwaiter. The storm troopers left, planning to return in the morning. This gave us a couple of hours to escape over the roofs of our four story house and neighboring buildings, fleeing for our lives in the dark of night.

## Four Long Years, Day to Day

Thus we entered an unknown world of hiding and escape, fear and agony. For the next four years I lost all I had, my entire family, home and belongings, and had to run from death and destruction, never knowing what the next day would bring, whether I would live or die. We hid out in many places, towns and cities, and each time our arrest seemed inevitable God seemed to put a hedge of angels around us. The longest time in one hideout was 212 days in one room: never going out except by crawling over the ground in the dark to be with my parents. They were hiding in the next house until they were betrayed by the woman who was hiding us—for 25 guilders each. That was the price the Nazis paid for information about Jews in hiding or anti-Germans listening to English radio broadcasts about the progress of the Allied forces. Alas, nothing had changed since Judas Iscariot!

I saw my dear parents rounded up and taken away with bayonets at their backs. They and my lovely younger brother, Eddie, who was betrayed some time later, were all murdered in concentration camps. The only thing Eddie had taken with him was his violin, which he played professionally. He was forced to play it while our people were being tormented and gassed. After the war I met a doctor who had survived, and told me about how the Germans kept Eddie without any medication as he suffered from typhoid and got to the point where his body could no longer cope with starvation. May God help them! It takes the love of Jesus to enable us to overcome and to want to forgive; to say "Father forgive them, for they know not what they do." We forgive, He heals the wounds, but the scars remain.

Space doesn't afford here for all that happened. But I can say that our God was in complete control and saw me through.

Even when I was held prisoner, having been arrested with a bayonet in my own back, God was there. He freed me right out of the "lion's den," forcing them to let me go in a most miraculous way!

**From Darkness to Light!**

When it seemed to us that our trials would never finish, finally the war came to an end. Suddenly, it seemed from all different directions people began to talk to me about Jesus. Then, I contacted a pastor who sent, believe it or not, a German lady to me. God does have a way with things! She had married an Orthodox Jewish man, become a Jewess, and lived a Jewish life for some 33 years. Her husband died suddenly leaving her brokenhearted and grieving much, but eventually she had found Jesus as her Messiah. For the next six weeks I argued with her about this Jesus, until she asked me to read Isaiah 53 and Psalm 22. Reading Isaiah 53, I did not understand a single word. Then, as promised, I started reading Psalm 22, and coming to verse 16 where it says "they pierced my hands and my feet," I let out one big yell, "Oh my, that is Jesus, because He was crucified!" I remembered all the Christian paintings I had seen years earlier in that church in Amsterdam, and suddenly all of it made sense. I went back to the 53rd chapter of Isaiah and now I understood each and every word. Hallelujah! The first thing I said was "it's like coming out of a dark hole into the light." Though I did not know it at that point, I found out later that Jesus is called "The Light of the World." As I read the Tanakh (Old Testament) all alone in a room, Yeshua revealed Himself to me: then and there I was born again. After reading the Gospels I understood even more.

Since those earlier days, God has not only furthered my concert career in the "New World," but He has enabled me to become a living testimony for Yeshua haMashiach

(Jesus the Messiah) as my personal Savior. Now, many years later, having been in Israel visiting the places where Yeshua walked and preached, the Word has become even more dear to me. Now it is no longer a dream, but my eyes have seen where He was, and how each day He is always near to us. Amen.

Life in the Shadow of the Swastika, *Frieda's book about her experience during WWII's Holocaust, including numerous close calls and miraculous escapes from the Nazis, is available from WMM and bookstores everywhere. Additionally, Frieda regularly shares her story of faith at speaking engagements around the world. Frieda's story is also available on audiocassette and CD. Please contact WMM for details.*

## In Search of Truth

David S. Taylor

My family comes from the Biblical tribe of Levi. Although I bear the last name of Taylor, my family name is originally Hochman. My father was born and raised an Orthodox Jew in Brooklyn, NY. As a professional musician, he played for many years with Guy Lombardo, and on the Ted Mack show. The name Taylor came about thus: in order to leave Poland and enter the Unites States, my grandfather assumed another person's identity, and chose the name 'Schneiderman.' Later my father chose the name Taylor (tailor in Yiddish is 'schneider') as a stage name, since "Sheldon Isadore Scheiderman" wasn't exactly a great stage name for a performer! Then, along came me.

I was raised in a traditional Jewish home and attended my synagogue weekly. Even at a young age, the synagogue services moved me; I felt a deep closeness to G-d, and desired to be a rabbi when I grew up. A Bar Mitzvah at 13, the rabbi worked with me within the instructions given to

101

him by my devoutly Orthodox grandfather. He must have been pleased at my ceremony as I remember lots of hugs and tears on that day. So I excelled in my early years.

The following year I was given my first job by my rabbi: to teach the beginner's Hebrew School class at my synagogue. Every Shabbat, I sat on the *bema* with my rabbi and the president of our synagogue, assisted removing and replacing the Torah scroll in the ark at the weekly readings. I continued to be very involved in my synagogue until I neared 16 years of age, at which time, I became more interested in playing guitar and hanging out with my friends. At 18 years of age I was earning a living as a guitar player in a band of 'music scholarship musicians' from a local college, and I decided music/entertainment would be my career.

During this time, my sister Debbie, who, like me, also had strong ties to our synagogue and our Jewish identity, told my family she believed in Jesus. Oy! Although I no longer attended synagogue and was far from G-d, I was shocked. I had a deep disdain for 'Christians' and especially towards Jesus, and I told her to never speak to me about Him.

During my early 20's, I became interested in Eastern philosophy, reading books by Carlos Casteneda, Krishnamurti and others, and also studied Korean martial arts, attaining a black belt in Tae Kwon Do. Still something was missing, and my interest in whether or not a "Supreme Being" really existed began to take hold of me. Somehow, I had the sense that a person, though sincere, could be wrong in their beliefs, and when they died end up in a place they wouldn't want to be.

One day, as I was walking on the beach, about to go surfing, I remember looking up to the sky and asking aloud, "If You are really there, please show me. The Christians say that Jesus is the only way, the Buddhists say Buddha is the enlightened one, this person says this, that person says that; how am I supposed to know? Whatever it is, I just want to know the truth because I don't want to be wrong."

My career as a musician continued, I was teaching martial arts, and at 23, I married my wife, Laurie. After year and a half I discovered that I didn't want all the responsibilities that came with marriage. I wanted out. I told Laurie that I wanted a divorce, but she was raised with strong values and didn't give in to my request. Unbeknownst to me, she began to cry out to God in prayer.

Our marriage continued to get worse, until one day I woke up and out of nowhere, this question popped into my head—"What IF Jesus is the Messiah?" As the day went on this question began to bother me to no end. As days passed, being the analytical person that I am, I began seriously considering what this meant and its ramifications. In fact, I became consumed with the prospect. I knew that if Jesus truly was the Messiah, then I, as a Jew, should believe in Him. If He really was the Messiah then whatever He said concerning this life, the world to come, and how to get there, had to hold the greatest weight of any words that have been spoken. But was He the Messiah, or not? I needed to know. Jesus was really bothering me.

One night I related this to Laurie, and I began asking her questions. She suggested I speak to my sister, Debbie. The next night Debbie and I went to work out at a local health club. When I saw her I said, "Debbie, Jesus is bothering me 24 hours a day. I can't get Him out of my head!"

She said to me, "David, I can prove to you that Jesus is our Messiah."

"If you can prove to me that Jesus is our Messiah from my Hebrew Bible," I said, "then I'll do whatever it takes to believe in Him. Just don't try to show me from your 'Christian Bible.' (I had always believed the Christians had changed the words in our Bible. I was actually scared of the 'red letter' passages I had seen.) Debbie proceeded to show me passages of Scripture from my Hebrew Bible. I was astounded!

I finished my workout and went to sit in the sauna. As I sat there, I reasoned to myself, on one hand, if I put my trust in Jesus, I stand to lose my family and friends; but, on the other hand—it was at this point clear to me from my own Hebrew Bible—He has to be the Jewish Messiah. At that moment I opted for Messiah. As I sat alone in a sauna at a martial arts center at 2 a.m., I confessed to G-d that I had gone my own way and not His; I had sinned against Him. I asked Jesus to come into my life. I told him that I believed He was my Messiah and that He rose from the dead on the third day.

Afterward I saw Debbie and said, "Well, I did it. This doesn't mean I have to start telling everyone about Jesus and go to a church, does it?" She just laughed.

The next day, I told Laurie what I had done. Later that week, Laurie also prayed and placed her faith in Messiah. As that week progressed, my life became radically different. Suddenly I saw Laurie in a way I had never experienced before—I had such a love for her. It was as though I was seeing her through someone else's eyes.

As I write this, we have been married for going on 25 years. This has been wonderful G-d's work in our lives. We have also been blessed with two wonderful children, Julie and Daniel, who have become Bar and Bat Mitzvah, and are also Jewish believers in Messiah with a strong sense of Jewish identity. We've been members of a Messianic Jewish congregation for 20 years, and I've been privileged to use the musical talent G-d gave me to serve as a worship leader. Over the years my love has deepened both for Yeshua and for my heritage as a Jew.

G-d answered the prayer I prayed on the beach over 20 years ago, for Him to show me the truth. I discovered that Truth is a Person, as Yeshua stated about Himself, "I am the way, the truth, and the life; no man comes to the Father but by Me." He has done a truly amazing work in my life, and for this I am eternally thankful.

## Still Jewish, Now I know Israel's Messiah!

Stacy Corrado

I was raised in a Conservative Jewish home in the greater Washington, DC area. I went through Hebrew school and was Bat-mitzvahed at the age of thirteen. Looking back now, I don't think I ever understood what it meant to have a relationship with God. I went through the motions, but never really understood why.

Fast-forward fifteen years where I now live: the "Bible Belt" of Charlotte, NC where most of my friends seem to be Christians (or at least Gentile). My two best friends, who are Christians, never really talked to me about what it meant to be a believer, but I could see they were absolutely amazing women. I thought they represented how a "Christian" should be: caring, truthful, dependable, loyal and not overbearing. But for some reason I actually appreciated the absence of faith in our conversations. Once, after a rather heated discussion with a friend about God, the Bible and eternal life, I decided to find out for myself what it was that I actually believed. I was so mad at her that I started reading anything I could on being Jewish, thinking to myself, " I am not going to buy into this 'Jesus thing.'" So I bought *The Idiot's Guide to the Bible* and read the entire book. At that point I started feeling like, "Well maybe this Jesus did do some pretty amazing things, if you actually believe it."

Then a friend invited me to her church where, as she explained, a Jewish man would be speaking. I accepted the invitation, and to my surprise, it was awesome. There was an amazing atmosphere of love and joy as I saw Jews and Gentiles worshiping the same God together. The speaker said that even if you believe in Yeshua, you are still Jewish. Well, this was a concept that I had never even considered. It reminded me of being able to get a ticket at the amusement park for that exciting ride I always thought I was too short for. After the service I told my two friends how interested I was in learning more. Though they did not show it, they were really excited. They later told me of all their prayers for me, how they had been praying for me "behind my back." I now thank God for them!

A few weeks later my friend took me to Hope of Israel Congregation. I found the service interesting and with Passover coming up I decided to celebrate with my family. I learned that Sam Nadler had written a *Messianic Passover Haggadah* that showed how Yeshua actually celebrated Passover. So I stopped by his office to get a copy to celebrate Passover that evening. Sam and I spoke briefly about what it meant to consider Yeshua as the Messiah of Israel, and Miriam actually offered to meet with me the following week to go over any questions. In my eyes, that was so generous that I eagerly accepted.

The next day was Saturday, and I decided to visit Hope of Israel Congregation again. How can I explain what the Lord did? When Sam invited those who wanted to accept Yeshua as Messiah, I prayed the sinners prayer. It was sort of like taking a bungee-jump and winning the lottery all at once! As I began to fully understand what had happened, I realized that not only was I still Jewish, but now I had the Messiah of Israel as well! Looking back, I see that I was 'born again' (John 3:3). Since then, my life has not been the same. Thank God for friends and their 'behind-the-back' prayers!

## A New Heart, A New Life

Gerry Lefkowitz

Though I went to synagogue growing up, I never found satisfaction and peace in religion, Jewish or otherwise. I was a 36-year-old Jewish man and my life was a complete disaster. I was now a drug addict, drowning in a sea of pornography, profanity, perversion and selfishness. My wife, daughter and I were all going in separate directions. The worst thing of all, though, was that my heart had become hardened, bitter, empty and getting worse day by day. I was incapable of giving or receiving love, and I was certain that my situation was hopeless. Little did I know that with the Lord, nothing is hopeless.

My wife, Maida, who had been a Gentile believer for three years, had been diligently praying for my salvation. Through her gentle and quiet spirit (1 Pet. 3:4), and the life of another Gentile man 'provoking me to jealousy' (Rom. 11: 11), I decided to try this "religion thing." That's when I met Yeshua, the Jewish Messiah. I admitted that I was a hopeless sinner and asked Him to come into my heart. I said to the Lord, "Yeshua, I can't help myself. I've tried almost everything except you. Everything I try seems to make it worse. Help me, Lord!" I said to Him, "Please do for me what You say You can do," and amazingly He did!

At the very moment of salvation, two amazing things happened to me. First, He removed that bitter, hardened

107

heart of stone, replaced it with a 'heart of flesh' (Ezek. 11:19; 36:26) delivering me from the just penalty for my sins (John 3:36).

Secondly, it seemed a faucet was turned on in my heart. Slowly at first, drop by drop, my empty heart began to be filled with faith, hope and love. Today, that faucet is a constant, steady stream.

Within two weeks of accepting the Lord, I was delivered from all of my 'outward sins.' That was seven years ago. My life is completely changed since I have received Yeshua. I can now freely give and receive love. I am a 'new creation' in Messiah with a heart burdened for lost souls: just as I use to be.

Though I'm constantly dependent on Messiah's grace and forgiveness, I'm now a Jewish believer who lives to study His Word, to follow His will, and to testify to His love. As Yeshua provides the opportunity, I hope to study to "show myself approved" and bring the message of Messiah to our people around the world, that they might know Shalom b'Yeshua: "Peace in Jesus", our Messiah.

## Finding the Faith of Abraham

Stewart Weinisch

I was raised in a traditional Jewish home. From the time I was nine years old until I was fourteen I attended Hebrew school, which stirred a desire to know God, and the truth about Him. At my Bar Mitzvah something 'deeper' occurred to me. I remember while looking into the ark where the Torahs were kept, I sensed I was missing something. There was a lot of religion, but there didn't seem to be any real faith. As I came to this conclusion, I made a promise to God, "Someday I will find the truth about who You are, and what You would require of me." Within a few months, however, I forgot my promise to God, and began to seek after the pleasures of the world. Although I was still practicing "being Jewish," God was the furthest thing from my mind.

A couple years later through a dating relationship with a Gentile believer in Jesus, I was challenged to consider what the Bible says about God and the purpose for my life. Plus, I had just lost my job, so I had lots of time on my hands. Over that year, we spent the majority of our time together reading the Bible. However, because I grew up believing that the New Testament was cursed, we focused only on the Hebrew Scriptures—specifically the Messianic prophecies. After a year of study and considering what I had read, I decided to visit a church. The pastor preached about the faith of Abraham (Gen. 15:6) and how Abraham was the 'father' of Jews and Christians, specifically the father of all those who believe in Yeshua (see Romans 4:11). I thought about this "faith", something I had pondered so long ago as a child, and realized in my heart this was something I didn't have.

Soon after this I took a look at the New Testament for the first time. Upon reading the very first verse, "A record of the genealogy of Yeshua the Messiah (Jesus Christ) the son of David, the son of Abraham…", I became convinced that if the Jewish people were going to have a Messiah, it had to be Jesus! It was then that I prayed to receive Yeshua as my Messiah and Lord, and I placed my trust in His atonement for my sins. Shortly after this, I sensed God working in my heart, and two things became very evident to me. First, I realized it was sort of an all or nothing deal—I had to love Him with my whole heart and live my life for Him, and second, I was going to bring the Good News of Messiah to my people.

Eventually, I met my wife Shoshannah, and God has blessed us with two wonderful children who love the Lord. To this day I continue to praise His Holy name for the privilege of knowing and serving Him, and for the opportunity to proclaim His name to my people.

## God's Love and A Life long Dream

Shoshannah Weinisch

I grew up in a middle-class Jewish family; by all outward appearances, my life has always been pleasant. But like many people, I found that the 'good life' was a myth. I was lonely in a family of six. My parents fought all the time and I never remember them ever saying that they loved me. When my mother left I took the role as 'mom,' but none of us were ever close. There was a haven for me, though: my great-grandfather's house. I would spend my summers there. His whole life revolved around synagogue and God. Though he didn't speak English, and I didn't speak Yiddish, I knew he loved me, and I knew God was in his home.

After high school, I went west to 'find myself.' I launched into a successful career at a high profile job with a computer related firm in California. Still, I was very, very lonely. I felt this big empty hole in my inner being that nothing could fill. I kept trying to fill it with relationships which ended up with me hurt and depressed. I pursued spirituality, knowledge, and philosophy, filled my hours with dancing, business, choreography, but I felt like I was being swallowed alive. People who saw me thought I had it all together. I looked busy and happy and successful. But I knew better. I knew I was dying.

Then things began to change. I found a Bible that someone had left in my apartment, and began to flip through it. For the first time, out of everything I had read, this made sense. I began to do what it talked about: turning the other cheek, humbling myself, etc., instead of beating people over the head. And it worked. I couldn't believe it! When I did things the way God said to do them it worked out for my benefit. This was real. Not only that, I was finally finding peace in my life.

Then one day as I was reading the Scriptures I realized there was a struggle going on inside of me, a power struggle, if you will. Could I commit my life to Yeshua? I got down on my knees by my bed and said, "God, if this is true—if Jesus if the Messiah—you've got to prove it supernaturally. It goes against everything I have been taught, and I can't do it on my own."

Within 24 hours my prayer was answered. When I went to pay my rent my landlady invited me in and initiated a conversation about the gospel—something she had never done. When I left—several hours later—I bumped into my neighbor, who for the first time began to share with me her beliefs that Jesus is the Messiah. Later at work I overheard some customers talking about Jesus. I spoke with them and they put me in touch with a Jewish believer. After we met to study the Scriptures a couple of times, I knew what I wanted. I wanted to please God. I wanted to belong to Him and have a relationship with Him. And I got what I wanted, and more! All my life I had wanted a husband devoted to me, and children. God has fulfilled the longings of my heart. I am truly amazed because there was no one further from God than me. But He forgave me, loved me, saved me. He's given me a family, my husband Stewart, and my children Melissa and Jonathan, and a life filled with Himself and His love. It's a life-long dream, and I'm living it every day!

# Smart, Successful, and Hopeless

Samuil Orman

I was born in Kiev, Ukraine. Both my parents are from Jewish families, and used to live in tsarist Russia, outside the city limits, in the Jewish *shtetl*, or village. My mom and dad were secular and we did not keep Jewish traditions. We lived ordinary lives, just like every one else. Raised with atheistic worldview, I later acquired a college degree, served in the Soviet Army, eventually married, and my wife and I had two daughters. I attained success in my career and reached the limits permissible for a Jew. As I looked at myself from the outside I was proud of my success, yet at the same time when I thought that life is going great, deep in my heart I felt empty and hopeless.

Nothing helped me: not books, films, TV/entertainment; not even spending time with friends. I now understand that at that time the Lord was beginning to work with the 'soil of my heart.' It was at this same time that I was asked to give a couple of lectures at my workplace on an atheistic subject. I agreed, but not with enthusiasm. I began to look for materials and to read books on this theme. Along with atheistic books and other material critical of the Bible, I wanted to read the Bible itself just to be accurate. In my circle of acquaintances there was a believer who brought me a Bible: it was the first Bible that I had ever had. I began to read it, but rather than being humbled by what I read, I became proud inside: I knew something that others did not know. I used this knowledge for self-satisfaction and did not connect it to the future, eternity and salvation.

One evening the phone rang, it was that believer. He invited me to the congregation. "Tomorrow Jews will preach at our meeting. Come, it will be interesting," he said. I was very surprised. "Jews preach in a church?" I thought, "How could that be?"

From the Bible I already knew that Jesus is a Jew. But growing up Jewish, I thought that Jesus was not for Jews. But I couldn't help wondering about this.

The next day I seemed to be drawn and I decided to go and hear what these Jewish men had to say about Jesus. On that morning it was raining, and it was as though somebody whispered to my ear, "Where are you going? It's cold, raining, the long way to go. You are not familiar with the route. Stay at home, there is a good show on TV." But I went. That day two Messianic Jews from the U.S. preached in the congregation: Sam Nadler was one of them. They shared their testimonies, talked about Yeshua, about Bible's prophecies. I was convinced about Yeshua. God did His job. I needed Him. When they asked to raise hands up of those who wanted to pray repentance prayer, I had no doubts in my heart that I was a sinner. I repented, believed in Yeshua and was born into a new life! That happened in April, 1989. On that day many other Jews got saved. The Lord gifted all of us with eternal life.

Since then I feel joy, knowing that I'm at peace with God. I know that from eternity God had decided to sow the seed of faith in my heart. He is holding me firmly in His hand, and someday I am going to meet Him: Yeshua my Savior!

## The Gift

Ella Orman

I was born in Kiev, Ukraine into a Jewish family. My parents did not raise me in a religious environment, but rather in the spirit of humanism. We did not talk about God, but we did talk about good and evil.

After completing general education I also graduated from university. Later I got married and considered myself very happy person, leading a pretty good life: loving husband, nice house, two daughters, interesting job, great friends, nothing seemed to be lacking. We owned really big book library that my husband had been collecting for many years. We loved to read and had a circle of friends that we got together with for discussions and book exchange. One day someone gave us a Bible as a gift. We were thrilled, since in our country that was a rare commodity, and it was very difficult to get one. I have to say that my husband read Bible mostly; I just could not find time to do it, yet I was very proud of the fact that we had a Bible in our home library.

One day my husband, Samuil, found out that in a congregation in Kiev, a Jewish man who believes in Yeshua would be speaking. He was very interested what he had to share and decided to visit that congregation.

That day began a new era in our lives. Samuil came back home very excited, he could not stop sharing what he heard. It had made such an impression on him that he came to believe in Yeshua.

I could not really understand what was happening, and I thought, "It's just a phase and it will pass soon." But I have to say that I saw many changes in him and his attitude. He was reading the Bible a lot and sharing with me what he was learning about the Lord.

Our interests began to differ since he came to faith in Yeshua, and that was really bothering me. One day, I decided to go with him to the congregation to see for myself what kind group that was. Shortly after my first visit, I also came to faith in One and Only Redeemer of Israel, Yeshua as my Messiah. From that time on we have studied and served the Lord together, and God has blessed our lives. A few years later we made *aliyah* to the Land of our Fathers, *Eretz Yisrael*, where we continue to share with our people the Good News of our loving Savior, Yeshua, the Shepherd of Israel!

# Finding Faith after 73 Years

Faith Eisler

I grew up in an Orthodox Jewish neighborhood in Brooklyn, NY. In those days the women did not attend the synagogue. Rather, we prepared for Shabbat (the Sabbath) and made sure the home and meals were ready when the men returned from services. My uncle in particular was very Orthodox and careful to obey all the rules for Shabbat, to the extent that we even 'pre-tore' the toilet paper for him to use on Saturday! But I never read or understood the Scriptures, because women did not need to understand or question religious matters. Consequently throughout my life I was never very religious, but I was always curious. In fact, just a few years ago when I was living in Las Vegas I asked an Orthodox Rabbi that I knew this question, "Rabbi, if Jesus was a Jew, why don't we as Jewish people revere Him?" He replied, "Because this Jesus was just a rebel rouser and nothing more." This remark left me bewildered and concerned. I couldn't understand 'why the Gentiles loved Yeshua so much, and why we as Jews had turned our backs on Him.'

A few years ago I moved to a retirement community near Winston-Salem, NC, to be nearer to my daughter. I realized very quickly that I didn't like my new living situation, but little did I realize that God would use this unlikely place to reveal Himself to me. This past Christmas season various church groups came and presented musical programs. As a Jewish woman I was not very interested in attending, but since one of the church groups included our maintenance man, Mark, I decided to attend this concert. "As the choir began singing their beautiful songs the music seemed to be reaching up to the heavens as they lifted their hands in praise. My heart was touched and to my surprise I found myself drawn to the music with tears rolling down my face." I later asked Mark, "I enjoyed the music so much, could I come and hear you again?" So Mark picked me up for his Sunday service on Christmas day and during the service my heart was drawn to the Lord.

I did not really understand everything that was happening, but after the service I went up for prayer and found myself telling the woman who was praying for me, "I believe in Jesus and I love Him." I felt God's peace and comfort, even though I was unsure as to how I as a Jewish woman could even admit such a thing.

As the weeks passed by, however, I began to doubt this new belief. More questions and doubts flooded my mind: What did I get myself into? How can I as a Jew believe in this Jesus? I'll never be welcomed in a synagogue again. My family will turn against me. How could I turn my back on my childhood teachings and my heritage? So even after I had prayed and trusted in Jesus these doubts from my past were plaguing me. I had many questions, and I was not experiencing the peace that I had at first. A few weeks later I moved to Charlotte where the manager of my new retirement community asked me if I would like to know about the synagogues in the area. I told him that I believed in Jesus and probably would not be comfortable in a traditional synagogue. "Well, there is a Messianic congregation in town where Jews believe in Jesus," he replied. I had never heard of such a thing and wondered if it could be true. Then I received a call from Miriam (Sam Nadler's wife), and she invited me to their services. In finding this community, God has truly answered my prayers!

*In 2006 Faith became a member of Hope of Israel Congregation, followed the Lord in believer's immersion, and publicly testified of her faith at her first Bat Mitzvah ceremony!*

# How I Came to Know My Messiah
Shari Belfer

I grew up in my Grandmother's home with my parents and older brother. It was an Orthodox Jewish home meaning we ate only Kosher food, and lit candles on Friday evening to welcome the Sabbath with the traditional challah bread and blessings over the home.

When I was six years old I begged my parents to allow me to attend Hebrew school. I loved learning the language though I was not taught the history behind my heritage. My Hebrew education lasted for six years. Most of my Jewish education was gained through living the traditions of my people. To be a good Jew, I learned to observe the Sabbath, eat no pork, attend synagogue, and on Rosh Hashanah and Yom Kippur, to pray to atone for all my sins.

As a child I attended the synagogue but also attended church occasionally with my Christian friends. I learned that Jesus was a Jewish carpenter, who traveled much to help people, to heal those that needed healing, performing miracles and eventually gave himself up to be crucified on the cross. I also learned that we Jews did not accept him as the Messiah to come. Rather, one day the Jewish Messiah would come and we would be lifted up and welcomed into heaven's gate to be with him. Still, I grew up wondering why Jesus was not our Messiah in general, and why He could not be my Messiah in particular.

At the age of 18, I met Mel. The following year we were married in an Orthodox Jewish ceremony. Mel was also raised in a traditional Jewish home and we tried to raise our two sons to love their heritage, having them Bar Mitzvahed in our local synagogue.

I worked all my adult life, except for the early years of raising our sons. I thought I would be a stay-at-home mom who would cook and take care of her family, watching my children grow up to become the wonderful adults they are today. However, God's plan for me was something else.

It turned out that at work I would have conversations about Jesus with an associate. Because of my interest my coworker went so far as to proclaim to me that in reality I was really a "closet Christian." In retrospect when I consider this time I realize that God was drawing me to Himself and I was being led to follow Him over those years.

One day in winter, through a door-to-door invitation to a Bible study in our Charlotte neighborhood, I found a small community of people who loved learning God's Word. This was something I had always desired and my husband and I were welcomed warmly as we discussed the issues of Scriptures each week. Knowing that we were Jewish, one of the women in the study invited us to the Hope of Israel Congregational Passover Banquet. It was at that Passover where I thought that perhaps Hope of Israel Congregation might be able to provide the spiritual answers and nurturing I longed for.

The next morning I attended their Shabbat services for the first time and felt like I had found my home. After a few weeks of attending the services I realized that Jesus is truly my Messiah and on April 25th 2009 I prayed to receive Him as my Savior.

When I told Mel he responded, "Well don't expect me to believe in Him, but you do as you please." Well, that was Mel's initial response, but after about a month of coming to services and having his own questions answered, Mel trusted in Messiah too!

Now, a full year and one Passover later, we are continuing to build our lives on the solid foundation of the Word of God. We have both been immersed and are serving members at Hope of Israel Congregation, continually growing there in discipleship. Throughout our lives, God has blessed Mel and me with beautiful children, grandchildren and friendships, and now we are complete in His peace, as even the Scriptures assure us (Romans 5:1).

## From the Land to the Lord

Henn Hetzroni, Interviewed by Matt Nadler

### How did you grow up?

I was born in Eilat, Israel. Soon after that time, my parents divorced and I went to live with my grandmother in Kiryat Malachi (City of Angels, in Southern Israel). There I went to a religious school. My grandmother was very traditional, keeping the Sabbath and going to synagogue. When my dad remarried, I moved in with him and switched to a secular school. At age 14, I moved to kibbutz Yad Mordechai while my parents stayed at Kiryat Malachi. I loved that time in my life, from twelve to 18. The kibbutz was secular; they weren't teaching about the Bible or God. Although they would not consider themselves against God, and even though they celebrated God's feasts - Shavuot, Rosh HaShanah and all that - they just did not believe in Him.

As far as my faith, even before my Bar Mitzvah, I began questioning God's existence, since He wouldn't answer my little challenges like, if you are real, make a horse appear. Also, to me, He wasn't a God to be loved, but feared. For example, in Israel we have high-rise buildings. Going from building to building, I would run, afraid that God was watching me. I thought that when I was inside the building I was okay, unexposed! This experience is imprinted in my memory.

119

In the kibbutz the emphasis was about the land, about loving your country, defending it for any price. I liked the idea of everyone coming together, being equal, doing activities which were patriotic. After that I went into the army (not by choice, of course).

**What about "Yeshua"?**

Yeshua? Yeshua, or Yeshu as we called him, was really more a curse-word, a derogatory term. For example if someone saw you eating meat and dairy together, one might say, "what are you... *notzri* (Christian) or something?"

Later on, I'd think that because he was from Natzeret, a carpenter, and heard things like this, I always thought of him as a person. Maybe he even existed. But he was just a man and people made him a god. That was my view then. I heard that he was Jewish, but I'd never read on it. It didn't interest me at all.

**And then you went into the army?**

Yes, I served three years. I was Givati [Brigade]. Within six months of me joining the army the first intifada started. It was the first time we had to deal with that kind of civilian warfare. I'd also been stationed in Lebanon, patrolling the northern border. I signed up for one more year and became an commander of a platoon. And that was enough.

**After that, you came to America.**

Yes, I came to the states, traveling with a friend. The plan was to go to South America, but my friend had to go back, so I was waiting for him. Two or three months later, I met Star [and her daughter Nicole] and we soon married.

Star was raised Christian, but at that time she wasn't a dedicated follower. Still, I remember we'd have arguments about evolution and God, though I didn't want to believe in "her side."

Now with the birth of Madisun our daughter and raising a family I felt like that we needed a solid value system for raising our daughters. At that time we were doing Shabbat dinner every Friday, the Jewish holidays, as well as the Christian ones, yet I did not realize at that time that I was praising and thanking God with my mouth [in the Shabbat blessings] and not my heart. I would go to synagogue every year on Yom Kippur to take care of the sins, but deep down I knew it was not sincere (on my part) - you'd go because that was the tradition.

Little by little, I actually started reading the Bible, but read nothing to do with Yeshua. I thought, Star can go with Jesus to God, whereas I can go to him direct. Same God, different ways.

### ..a direct line?

(laughs) Yeah, whereas she needed a middle man. But, I'd think, we all praise the same God, so no big deal.

### What changed?

Star was becoming more committed to the Lord and she and Madisun began attending a church. And I am thinking, okay? This is a change. But I also thought, I am the father. I need to go as the man of the house, as a family. So I went with them to services.

The services were not the Catholic rituals I was expecting. The whole thing kind of fit. Afterward they'd have an oneg, a time of getting together. I realized they had a peacefulness and a love for each other. I also started reading the New Covenant, as I was attending services. The message of the text surprised me by its Jewishness.

### How so?

Well, even the names, and the places - most of all the places. Jerusalem, Jaffa, Jordan ... Israel. And I started to realize that this Jesus was a man who cared for people around him, He was not someone who just said "believe in me," and that's it, which is how he had been portrayed to me.

At the same time, I thought, well, I am Jewish, but this is Christian. I couldn't understand the theology of it all. When we eventually moved to Charlotte, we started going to Lakeshore Christian Fellowship, and I continued to learn about Jesus. But still, how could I believe? What about all the Jewish holidays - what about my heritage? So in my view I was going to services for *shalom bayit* (peace in the family), just as they would have Hanukkah and such for me.

Eventually Star and I had a talk about the two directions of faith our family was taking. She encouraged me to consider who Jesus was. Later, while on business in Houston, I was feeling convicted, yet afraid. Again, I didn't know how to believe. So I called Pastor Gil of Lakeshore [Christian Fellowship], and he assured me that, far from becoming a Gentile, I would be a testimony for Yeshua to the Jewish people by remaining Jewish. I went to God and confessed my sins, confessing Yeshua as my Lord and Savior. It was a new page. Though I saw all my sins, my shame, and could not imagine how God could forgive me, He did. I was a different person.

The next day, I was hungry for the Scriptures. I would read and study, getting revelation and answers left and right. Studying and praying confirmed to me I was on the right path.

Even before that, Sam [Nadler] had come to our church - I was not there, but Star had told me about it. He did a seder. And she said, "Henn I really think you should talk to this guy. He showed how Jesus... he is your Messiah more than anything." This was before I had come to faith. And she proceeded to explain to me elements of the seder, from his message. So I listened to the podcast and was surprised.

Eventually, after becoming a believer, Pastor Gil encouraged me to go to Hope of Israel so that our family could live in a Messianic Jewish context. Months later, doubts crept in as I began to realize I would have to tell my parents. I wondered again at how faith in Yeshua could be real.

Finally I told them, when they came to visit from Israel. I was anxious about their response. At first they didn't understand the concept totally, though they knew something had changed for the better. It was around Yom Yerushalayim (in May) that they visited Hope of Israel. When they came to service, they cried. They teared up at the songs about Jerusalem, the dancing, etc. They could see that we were a part of the Jewish people - and they were happy for me. My mom looked at me and said to me, "I am proud of you." I thought it would be the worst! But they were really good about it. My mom even said, "if every synagogue in Israel would be like this - we would have a lot of the youth following God!"

I see what my parents meant, too: many of the customs that I just did without meaning, now have life in my Messiah.

***When I heard you give your story to the youth, you described how your family life was different now.***

Oh yeah, for my immediate family? Absolutely. Now we walk with meaning. We put Him first, and it makes life easier in a sense, in that we understand how things line up under Him. Any issue that we have, we bring it to the Lord we pray and read the Scriptures. For example if I instruct Madisun in something I base it according to the Bible and it's authority. It is His word, not ours. We can ask, "how will this look in the eyes of the Lord"?

We live an everyday life with accountability to God. I am so grateful for having the Lord in my life. He is a good God, and there's a purpose to it all.

52:13 Behold, My servant will prosper, He will be high and lifted up and greatly exalted.

14 Just as many were astonished at you, My people, so His appearance was marred more than any man and His form more than the sons of men.

15 Thus He will sprinkle many nations, and kings will shut their mouths on account of Him; for what had not been told them they will see, and what they had not heard they will understand.

53:1 Who has believed our report? And to whom has the arm of the Lord been revealed?

2 For He shall grow up before Him as a tender plant, and as a root out of dry ground. He has no form or comeliness; and when we see Him, there is no beauty that we should desire Him.

3 He is despised and rejected by men, a Man of sorrows and acquainted with grief. And we hid, as it were, our faces from Him; He was despised, and we did not esteem Him.

4 Surely He has borne our griefs and carried our sorrows; yet we esteemed Him stricken, smitten by God, and afflicted.

5 But He was wounded for our transgressions, He was bruised for our iniquities; the chastisement for our peace was upon Him, and by His stripes we are healed.

6 All we like sheep have gone astray; we have turned, every one, to his own way; And the Lord has laid on Him the iniquity of us all.

7 He was oppressed and He was afflicted, yet He opened not His mouth; He was led as a lamb to the slaughter, and as a

52:13 הִנֵּה יַשְׂכִּיל עַבְדִּי יָרוּם וְנִשָּׂא וְגָבַהּ מְאֹד:

52:14 כַּאֲשֶׁר שָׁמְמוּ עָלֶיךָ רַבִּים כֵּן־מִשְׁחַת מֵאִישׁ מַרְאֵהוּ
וְתֹאֲרוֹ מִבְּנֵי אָדָם:

52:15 כֵּן יַזֶּה גּוֹיִם רַבִּים עָלָיו יִקְפְּצוּ מְלָכִים פִּיהֶם
כִּי אֲשֶׁר לֹא־סֻפַּר לָהֶם רָאוּ וַאֲשֶׁר לֹא־שָׁמְעוּ הִתְבּוֹנָנוּ:

53:1 מִי הֶאֱמִין לִשְׁמֻעָתֵנוּ וּזְרוֹעַ יְיָ עַל־מִי נִגְלָתָה:

53:2 וַיַּעַל כַּיּוֹנֵק לְפָנָיו וְכַשֹּׁרֶשׁ מֵאֶרֶץ צִיָּה
לֹא־תֹאַר לוֹ וְלֹא הָדָר
וְנִרְאֵהוּ וְלֹא־מַרְאֶה וְנֶחְמְדֵהוּ:

53:3 נִבְזֶה וַחֲדַל אִישִׁים אִישׁ מַכְאֹבוֹת וִידוּעַ חֹלִי
וּכְמַסְתֵּר פָּנִים מִמֶּנּוּ נִבְזֶה וְלֹא חֲשַׁבְנֻהוּ:

53:4 אָכֵן חֳלָיֵנוּ הוּא נָשָׂא וּמַכְאֹבֵינוּ סְבָלָם
וַאֲנַחְנוּ חֲשַׁבְנֻהוּ נָגוּעַ מֻכֵּה אֱלֹהִים וּמְעֻנֶּה:

53:5 וְהוּא מְחֹלָל מִפְּשָׁעֵנוּ מְדֻכָּא מֵעֲוֹנֹתֵינוּ
מוּסַר שְׁלוֹמֵנוּ עָלָיו וּבַחֲבֻרָתוֹ נִרְפָּא־לָנוּ:

53:6 כֻּלָּנוּ כַּצֹּאן תָּעִינוּ אִישׁ לְדַרְכּוֹ פָּנִינוּ
וַיְיָ הִפְגִּיעַ בּוֹ אֵת עֲוֹן כֻּלָּנוּ:

53:7 נִגַּשׂ וְהוּא נַעֲנֶה וְלֹא יִפְתַּח־פִּיו כַּשֶּׂה לַטֶּבַח יוּבָל
וּכְרָחֵל לִפְנֵי גֹזְזֶיהָ נֶאֱלָמָה וְלֹא יִפְתַּח פִּיו:

sheep before its shearers is silent, so He opened not His mouth.

8 He was taken from prison and from judgment, And who will declare His generation? For He was cut off from the land of the living; for the transgressions of My people He was stricken.

9 And they made His grave with the wicked -- but with the rich at His death, because He had done no violence, nor was any deceit in His mouth.

10 Yet it pleased the LORD to bruise Him; He has put Him to grief. When You make His soul an offering for sin, He shall see His seed, He shall prolong His days, and the pleasure of the LORD shall prosper in His hand.

11 He shall see the labor of His soul, and be satisfied. By His knowledge My righteous Servant shall justify many, for He shall bear their iniquities.

12 Therefore I will divide Him a portion with the great, and He shall divide the spoil with the strong, because He poured out His soul unto death, and He was numbered with the transgressors, and He bore the sin of many, and made intercession for the transgressors.

53:8 מֵעֹ֤צֶר וּמִמִּשְׁפָּט֙ לֻקָּ֔ח וְאֶת־דּוֹר֖וֹ מִ֣י יְשׂוֹחֵ֑חַ
כִּ֤י נִגְזַר֙ מֵאֶ֣רֶץ חַיִּ֔ים מִפֶּ֥שַׁע עַמִּ֖י נֶ֥גַע לָֽמוֹ׃

53:9 וַיִּתֵּ֤ן אֶת־רְשָׁעִים֙ קִבְר֔וֹ וְאֶת־עָשִׁ֖יר בְּמֹתָ֑יו
עַ֚ל לֹא־חָמָ֣ס עָשָׂ֔ה וְלֹ֥א מִרְמָ֖ה בְּפִֽיו׃

53:10 וַֽיהוָ֞ה חָפֵ֤ץ דַּכְּאוֹ֙ הֶֽחֱלִ֔י
אִם־תָּשִׂ֤ים אָשָׁם֙ נַפְשׁ֔וֹ יִרְאֶ֥ה זֶ֖רַע יַאֲרִ֣יךְ יָמִ֑ים
וְחֵ֥פֶץ יְהוָ֖ה בְּיָד֥וֹ יִצְלָֽח׃

53:11 מֵעֲמַ֤ל נַפְשׁוֹ֙ יִרְאֶ֣ה יִשְׂבָּ֔ע
בְּדַעְתּ֗וֹ יַצְדִּ֤יק צַדִּיק֙ עַבְדִּ֔י לָֽרַבִּ֑ים וַעֲוֺנֹתָ֖ם ה֥וּא יִסְבֹּֽל׃

53:12 לָכֵ֞ן אֲחַלֶּק־ל֣וֹ בָֽרַבִּ֗ים וְאֶת־עֲצוּמִים֮ יְחַלֵּ֣ק שָׁלָל֒
תַּ֗חַת אֲשֶׁ֨ר הֶעֱרָ֤ה לַמָּ֙וֶת֙ נַפְשׁ֔וֹ וְאֶת־פֹּשְׁעִ֖ים נִמְנָ֑ה
וְהוּא֙ חֵטְא־רַבִּ֣ים נָשָׂ֔א וְלַפֹּשְׁעִ֖ים יַפְגִּֽיעַ׃ ס

## PROPHECIES OF THE MESSIAH

"We have found Him of whom Moses in the Law and also the Prophets spoke - Yeshua of Nazareth" (John 1:45)

| Subject | Old Covenant | New Covenant |
|---|---|---|
| A descendent of Abraham | Genesis 12:3 | Matthew 1:1 Galatians 3:8 |
| Of the Tribe of Judah | Genesis 49:10 | Luke 3:33 |
| Heir of King David | Isaiah 9:7 | Luke 1:32 |
| He was to come before the destruction of the Temple | Malachi 3:1 Daniel 9:26 | Matthew 24:1 |
| He was to be born in Bethlehem | Micah 5:2(1) | Luke 2:4-7 |
| Born of a virgin | Isaiah 7:14 | Matthew 1:23 |
| A ministry in Galilee | Isaiah 9:1(8:23) | Matthew 4:13-16 |
| Son of God | Psalm 2:7,12 | Matthew 3:17 |
| He is God in the flesh | Isaiah 9:6(5); 10:21 | Hebrews 1:8-12 |
| Preceded by a forerunner | Isaiah 40:3 Malachi 3:1 | Mark 1:2-4 |
| Initially rejected by His people | Isaiah 53:3 | John 1:11 |
| He was to be an atonement for sins | Isaiah 53:6 Daniel 9:24-26 | Matthew 20:28 |
| He was resurrected | Psalm 16:10 | Luke 24:6-7 |
| He will be accepted | Zechariah 12:10 | Revelation 1:7 |

*Messianic Foundations: Fulfill Your Calling in the Jewish Messiah* - offers a vision of Messianic faith motivated by the testimony that Yeshua is God's faithfulness to Israel.

*Messiah in the Feasts of Israel* - explores the Biblical feasts in light of Yeshua, from Passover to Sukkot, and more!

*Messianic Discipleship: Following Yeshua, Growing in Messiah* - leads the reader through a Jewish discipleship course, dealing with the essentials of Messianic faith.

*Even You Can Share The Jewish Messiah* - a short booklet with key information on sharing Yeshua with friends and neighbors, even "to the Jew first" (Romans 1:16).

*The Messianic Passover Haggadah* - the perfect guide for conducting your own Passover *seder*.

*Messianic Wisdom: Practical Scriptural Answers for Your Life* - get a grasp on Messianic Jewish issues and living out your faith in Messiah.

*Messianic Life Lessons from the Book of Ruth* - an in-depth, information-rich devotional commentary on this priceless book of restoration from the Tanakh.

*Messianic Life Lessons from the Book of Jonah* - a rich, accessible commentary on this book about Israel's mission to the Gentiles.

*Abiding in Messiah* by Miriam Nadler - devotional teachings on bearing fruit in Yeshua.

*Honoring God With My Life* by Miriam Nadler - this expositional study of Titus 2:3-5 is perfect for women's studies and all those seeking to live out God's purpose.

For more information, please call or write

Word of Messiah Ministries

PO Box 79238

Charlotte, NC 28271

704-544-1948

The Messianic Answer Book,

Revised Edition

Copyright © 2008

Eighth Printing 2016

ISBN 0-9702619-0-X

Made in the USA
Columbia, SC
09 May 2020